Worth Tasting

Worth Tasting

A Culinary Tour Through the
Architecture of the Palm Beaches

The Junior League of the Palm Beaches is an organization of women committed to promoting voluntarism, developing the potential of women, and improving communities through the effective action and leadership of trained volunteers. Its purpose is exclusively educational and charitable.

Worth Tasting
A Culinary Tour Through the Architecture of the Palm Beaches

Published by The Junior League of the Palm Beaches, Inc.
470 Columbia Drive, Building F
West Palm Beach, Florida 33409
561.689.7590

Library of Congress Control Number: 2006934743
ISBN: 978-0-9608090-2-8

Edited, Designed, and Manufactured by
Favorite Recipes® Press
An imprint of

FRP

P. O. Box 305142
Nashville, Tennessee 37230
800.358.0560

Art Director: Steve Newman
Book Design: Starletta Polster
Project Manager and Editor: Debbie Van Mol

Manufactured in China
First Printing 2007 12,500 copies

The proceeds from the sale of *Worth Tasting* will be reinvested in the community through the projects and programs of The Junior League of the Palm Beaches.

Other books published by The Junior League of the Palm Beaches:
   Palm Beach Entertains
   Heart of the Palms
   Slice of Paradise

To purchase additional copies of this cookbook or any of the previously published cookbooks, please call 561.689.7590, or visit us at our Web site www.jlpb.org. Order information is located on page 176.

Preface

The members of The Junior League of the Palm Beaches, Inc., are proud to share our fourth cookbook with you, *Worth Tasting: A Culinary Tour Through the Architecture of the Palm Beaches*. Florida's Palm Beaches has a rich and colorful history and conjures up images of beautiful sunrises, tropical beaches, luxurious living, and stunning architecture. The famous Worth Avenue on Palm Beach offers fine dining, extraordinary international boutiques and specialty shops, and an inviting ocean side setting. In *Worth Tasting*, you will be transported to the beautiful Palm Beaches on a veritable journey of the senses. You will enjoy not only treasured recipes, but beautiful color photography by Gregory Ross. He has captured the essence, beauty, and charm of a select number of the buildings that characterize the Palm Beaches. In addition, you will discover interesting history, cooking tips, menus, and fun facts from events held at several of the distinguished venues featured in this cookbook. Enjoy your culinary and architectural journey through the pages that follow. We are certain you will find that the recipes are indeed "worth tasting!"

In 1941, The Junior League of the Palm Beaches began the legacy of promoting voluntarism, developing the potential of women, and improving the community through the effective action and leadership of trained volunteers. For more than sixty-five years, The Junior League of the Palm Beaches has fulfilled this mission. Since its founding, our League has contributed $3 million to community projects. In the past ten years alone, our members have collectively contributed more than 325,000 volunteer hours to the community. Proceeds from *Worth Tasting* support the community projects of The Junior League of the Palm Beaches, making our community a better place for all who live here. Over the years, The Junior League of the Palm Beaches has partnered with many organizations in Palm Beach County, some of which include the Crippled Children's Society, the Norton Museum of Art, Head Start, The Susan G. Komen Foundation, the Armory Arts Center, Mounts Botanical Garden, the Historical Society of Palm Beach County, the Literacy Coalition, and the Nicklaus Children's Hospital. In the 1950s, The Junior League of the Palm Beaches founded the Junior Museum, which later became the South Florida Science Museum, one of the top attractions in Palm Beach County. In the late 1990s, the League was instrumental as a founding partner in bringing Quantum House to the campus of St. Mary's Medical Center. Quantum House serves as a hospitality house for families with seriously ill children and provides families with comfortable lodging and emotional support. The Junior League of the Palm Beaches specializes in community partnerships and helps to build valuable community resources with a corps of trained women volunteers.

In order to continue giving time, talent, and treasure to the residents of the Palm Beaches in such a significant way, our League has strived to create a fabulous cookbook that you, its readers, will treasure and that will bring fund-raising dollars to those in need in our community. We are women building better communities, and we wholeheartedly thank you for your support.

Tastefully Yours,

Mary Reynolds
2005–2006 President

Amy Triggs
2006–2007 President

Jodi L. Chapin
2007–2008 President

The Junior League of the Palm Beaches

Contents

Introduction

Palm Beach County is both a historical and an architectural phenomenon, and people from all over the nation are drawn to its "mystique." As cookbooks have become historical through the years, they are wonderful tools not only for cooking, but also for giving us insight into the people and culture from the place where they are produced. *Worth Tasting: A Culinary Tour Through the Architecture of the Palm Beaches* does just that. The recipes in this book reveal the friendliness, creativity, talent, and hospitable nature of our Palm Beach County citizens through simple, traditional, elegant, and even "trendy" ideas and menus. Each chapter highlights a site with historical significance to Palm Beach County, as well as providing delicious recipes that you will enjoy sharing with friends.

It has been said that, "A good dinner sharpens wit, while it softens the heart." That is what this cookbook is all about. Especially delightful is that the proceeds from the sales of this cookbook will be returned to the community to support many worthwhile Junior League projects!

As you begin to leaf through the book and dream about the fabulous menus outlined in it, you will remember words we have all spoken: "God is great. God is good. Let us thank Him for this food. Amen."

Barbara Nicklaus

Barbara Nicklaus
The Junior League of the Palm Beaches Sustainer

Cookbook Committee

Chair
Esther Uria LaBovick

Assistant Chair
Kimberly Lyon

RECIPES
Deborah Sutera—*Chair*
Erin Galloway
Catherine Hennessey
Jennifer Morrison

DESIGN
Denise A. Bas—*Chair*
Kate Merrell
Julia Pichette
Kelly Tracht
Kelly White

MARKETING
Kimberly Lyon—*Chair*

Patricia Admire
Beth Beattie
Aime Dunstan
Ann Gagliardi
Stirling Clarke Halversen
Catherine Hennessey
Nicole Miller Jablonski
Christina Jerabek
Sarah Kauss

Martha Gabriel Klein
Kara Koch
Kate Merrell
Jennifer Morrison
Joanne O'Connor
Eileen O'Malley
Robyn O'Reilly
Julia Pichette
Sarah White

APPETIZERS & BEVERAGES

The Harriet Himmel Theater

The Harriet Himmel Theater for Cultural and Performing Arts is one of West Palm Beach's newest state-of-the-art theaters. Transformed from a historical church, Harriet Himmel is at the heart of downtown CityPlace.

The First United Methodist Church of the Palm Beaches laid the first cornerstone on May 2, 1926. Walker Brothers of Birmingham, Alabama, built the three-story 51,786-square-foot building at a cost of $225,000. The Spanish Colonial Revival architecture was designed by Spencer and Phillips of Memphis, Tennessee. The church's main sanctuary includes significant architectural elements, such as open-tress cypress ceilings and large divided windows that overlook the main floor. The wide exterior entrance steps direct guests into the white stucco building's entrance hall. The main lobby is flanked by staircases that lead to the tiered mezzanine. The church congregation celebrated the first service on Christmas Eve 1926, under the direction of the Reverend L. M. Broyles.

The Methodist church opened its doors for worshipers while welcoming the Palm Beach community, including victims from the 1928 hurricane. The victims were able to remain in the church's shelter until their homes were rebuilt eleven months later. Unable to recover from the Crash of 1929, the church was forced to turn the deed back to the bondholders and conduct services in a local school. When the bondholders could not secure a buyer, the church was offered the building for $25,000. Willing to sell even wedding rings to raise the money, the church congregation was able to regain ownership of the beloved building.

The subsequent $2.75 million sale of the church turned ownership over to the Downtown/Uptown developers Henry Rolfs and David Paladino. The last church service was held on New Years Eve 1989. The United Methodist Church relocated to an $8 million sanctuary on Brandywine Road in West Palm Beach. Renovations on the building began in late 1998 under the direction of Palladium at CityPlace. The building was transformed into an 11,000-square-foot cultural arts center. The building was renamed The Harriet Himmel Theater in honor of Mrs. Himmel's generous donation to complete the restoration. The revitalization included the installation of an exterior clock and the reconstruction of the four-story bell tower. The bell rang for the CityPlace opening in October of 2000. The Harriet Himmel Theater is in the center of outdoor shopping, fine dining, and entertainment, and serves as a venue for the performing arts, exhibits, seminars, social events, and even Sunday morning services. Throughout the decades and architectural alterations, The Harriet Himmel Theater has remained a treasured landmark in the daily and social lives of both residents and visitors of Palm Beach County.

Cocktail Party

RASPBERRY MOJITOS

BLOODY MARY SHRIMP SHOOTERS

ASPARAGUS AND PROSCIUTTO ROLLS

SAUTÉED APPLES WITH GOAT CHEESE

UPTOWN FROMAGE

KALAMATA OLIVE TAPENADE

CRAB CLAWS COCONUT

WHISKEY CAKE

Pinot Noir, California or Oregon *

* see page 170

TEXAS PEPPER PECANS

1/4	cup butter, melted	1/2	teaspoon seasoned salt
1	tablespoon Worcestershire sauce	1/2	teaspoon salt
1 1/2	teaspoons Tabasco sauce	1/4	teaspoon pepper
1/2	teaspoon garlic salt	1	pound pecan halves

Combine the butter, Worcestershire sauce, Tabasco sauce, garlic salt, seasoned salt, salt and pepper in a large bowl and mix well. Add the pecans to the butter mixture and stir until coated.

Spread the pecans in a single layer in a 10×15-inch baking pan. Bake at 350 degrees for 20 to 25 minutes or until light brown, stirring halfway through the baking process. Remove to a platter to cool. Store in a sealable plastic bag. Quick and easy appetizer for a cocktail party or impromptu gathering.

MAKES 2 CUPS

Did you know? Jane Dahlmeier, contributor of the recipe Texas Pepper Pecans, is a Junior League of the Palm Beaches sustainer and has contributed to both of the previous League cookbooks, Slice of Paradise *and* Heart of the Palms.

ASPARAGUS AND PROSCIUTTO ROLLS

36	small fresh asparagus spears, trimmed and blanched	2	tablespoons minced fresh chives
			Salt and pepper to taste
1/3	cup olive oil	6	slices prosciutto, cut lengthwise into halves
2	tablespoons balsamic vinegar		
1	tablespoon spicy Dijon mustard	6	tablespoons goat cheese
2	garlic cloves, crushed		

Cut the asparagus spears into 4-inch lengths. Whisk the olive oil, vinegar, Dijon mustard and garlic in a bowl until combined. Stir in the chives and season with salt and pepper.

Arrange the prosciutto halves on a sheet of waxed paper. Spread a 1-inch border of the goat cheese along one edge of each prosciutto half. Layer each prosciutto half with three asparagus spears and roll tightly to enclose the filling. Arrange seam side down on a serving platter and drizzle with the olive oil vinaigrette. Garnish with fresh parsley. Serve at room temperature.

SERVES 6

WORTH TASTING

CHERRY TOMATO AND OLIVE BRUSCHETTA

10 ounces assorted cherry tomatoes
    (yellow, tige and cherry)
Handful of pitted black olives, mashed
4 to 5 tablespoons extra-virgin olive oil
Handful of fresh basil, torn
Herb vinegar to taste
1 dried chile, crushed

1 tablespoon dried oregano
Sea salt and freshly ground pepper to taste
1 loaf French or rustic bread,
    thickly sliced and toasted
$^1/_2$ garlic clove, minced
Shaved Parmesan cheese

Mash the tomatoes in a bowl and stir in the olives. Add the olive oil, basil, vinegar, chile and oregano and mix well. Season with salt and pepper.

Rub both sides of the toasted bread slices with the garlic. Spoon the tomato mixture on the bread slices and sprinkle with cheese. Arrange on a serving platter and serve immediately.

SERVES 4

GRILLED LEMON BRUSCHETTA

2 tablespoons extra-virgin olive oil
2 tablespoons fresh lemon juice
1 teaspoon chopped fresh
    rosemary
Salt to taste

6 ($^1/_2$x3$^1/_2$-inch) slices white rustic
    bread, cut into halves
1 large garlic clove, cut into halves
1 teaspoon grated lemon zest
Freshly ground pepper to taste

Whisk the olive oil, lemon juice and rosemary in a bowl until combined. Season with salt.

Heat a grill pan over medium-high heat. Grill the bread slices on the hot grill pan for 2 minutes per side or until golden brown. Rub both sides of the warm toasted bread slices with the garlic and brush with the olive oil mixture. Sprinkle with the lemon zest, salt and pepper. Arrange the bruschetta on a long narrow platter and garnish with lemon slices. If desired, use a countertop electric kitchen grill, or for a more authentic flavor, grill over hot coals.

SERVES 6

SAUTÉED APPLES WITH GOAT CHEESE

1	baguette	4	or 5 green apples, sliced
1/4	cup olive oil		(Fuji or Granny Smith)
Kosher salt and pepper to taste		2	tablespoons apple vodka
1	tablespoon butter	2	cups plus 3 tablespoons crumbled
			goat cheese, softened

Slice the baguette into thirty-five rounds. Brush both sides of each round with some of the olive oil and sprinkle lightly with salt and pepper. Arrange the slices cut side up on a baking sheet.

Melt the butter in a small saucepan. Add the apple slices and toss to coat. Stir in the vodka and cook for 3 minutes or until the apples are tender-crisp, stirring frequently. Remove from the heat.

Arrange 1 apple slice on each round and spoon 1 tablespoon of the goat cheese on each apple slice. Broil on low until light brown and serve immediately. For added flavor, add dried cranberries to the cooked apple mixture, or use a sweetened goat cheese such as cranberry walnut goat cheese.

MAKES 35

GOAT CHEESE is lower in fat and cholesterol than cow's cheese. It is easier to digest because the fat cells in goat cheese are smaller and break down more easily. Many people who are lactose intolerant can still eat goat cheese without a problem. Feta goat cheese is cured in brine and is very salty. As a result, it is not recommended to substitute feta cheese for goat cheese unless you want a saltier outcome.

SAVORY ARTICHOKE SPINACH DIP

1	(10-ounce) package frozen chopped spinach, thawed and drained	1 1/2	cups (6 ounces) shredded Monterey Jack cheese
1	(14-ounce) can artichoke hearts, drained and finely chopped	2	cups mayonnaise
		2	garlic cloves, crushed
1 1/2	cups (6 ounces) shredded Parmesan cheese	2	teaspoons Tabasco sauce
		Paprika to taste	

Press the excess moisture from the spinach. Combine the spinach, artichokes, Parmesan cheese, Monterey Jack cheese, mayonnaise, garlic and Tabasco sauce in a bowl and mix well.

Spoon the artichoke mixture into a 2-quart baking dish and sprinkle with paprika. Bake at 350 degrees for 30 minutes. Serve warm with assorted party crackers and/or crudités.

SERVES 12

WORTH TASTING

HOT ARTICHOKE CRAB DIP

1	(14-ounce) can artichoke hearts, drained and chopped	1/2	cup (2 ounces) shredded mozzarella cheese
1	(6-ounce) jar marinated artichoke hearts, drained and chopped	1	cup light mayonnaise
1	(6-ounce) can crab meat, drained and flaked	1	teaspoon garlic powder
1	cup (4 ounces) grated Parmesan cheese		Worcestershire sauce to taste

Combine the artichoke hearts, crab meat, Parmesan cheese and mozzarella cheese in a bowl and mix gently. Fold in the mayonnaise, garlic powder and Worcestershire sauce.

Spoon the crab meat mixture into a 1-quart baking dish and bake at 350 degrees for 25 to 30 minutes or until heated through. Serve warm with crostini.

SERVES 20

CREAMY HERB CRAB DIP

1	cup plain 1% yogurt	1	tablespoon chopped fresh dill weed
6	ounces fresh or canned crab meat, drained and flaked	1	teaspoon fresh lemon juice
1/4	cup light mayonnaise	1/4	teaspoon freshly cracked pepper
		1/8	teaspoon hot red pepper sauce

Combine the yogurt, crab meat, mayonnaise, dill weed, lemon juice, cracked pepper and hot sauce in a bowl and mix well. Chill, covered, for up to one day. Serve with assorted party crackers and/or fresh vegetables. Add a small amount of wasabi for a spicier flavor.

MAKES 1 1/4 CUPS

WORTH TASTING

AVOCADO BEAN DIP

1	(15-ounce) can garbanzo beans, drained and rinsed
1	(15-ounce) can black beans, drained and rinsed
1	(11-ounce) can white Shoe Peg corn, drained and rinsed
1	(10-ounce) can tomatoes with green chiles
2	avocados, chopped
2	garlic cloves, minced
1	tablespoon chopped fresh cilantro
1	teaspoon seasoned salt

Mix the beans and corn in a large serving bowl. Partially drain the tomatoes and stir the remaining undrained tomatoes into the bean mixture. Add the avocados, garlic, cilantro and seasoned salt and mix gently. Serve with corn chips.

SERVES 12

HOT BACON AND SWISS DIP

8	ounces cream cheese, softened
1	cup (4 ounces) shredded Swiss cheese
1/2	cup mayonnaise
2	tablespoons chopped green onions
10	slices bacon, crisp-cooked and crumbled
1/2	cup (or more) butter cracker crumbs

Combine the cream cheese, Swiss cheese, mayonnaise and green onions in a mixing bowl and beat until combined. Spoon the cheese mixture into a 1-quart baking dish and sprinkle with the bacon. Cover with the cracker crumbs. Bake at 350 degrees for 30 minutes or until bubbly. Serve warm with butter crackers.

SERVES 8 TO 10

WORTH TASTING

SAVORY CHEESE DIP

12 ounces Jarlsburg cheese, shredded
2   cups mayonnaise
2   cups sliced onions

Combine the cheese, mayonnaise and onions in a bowl and mix well. Spoon the cheese mixture into a baking dish. Bake at 350 degrees for 25 minutes. Serve warm with Triscuits.
SERVES 8

PESTO-GOAT CHEESE DIP

8   ounces goat cheese
1   (7-ounce) container pesto
2   (1-ounce) packages pine nuts
1   tomato, chopped

Spread the goat cheese over the bottom of a 10-inch baking dish. Spread the pesto over the goat cheese and sprinkle with the pine nuts and tomato. Bake at 350 degrees for 25 minutes. Serve warm with assorted party crackers.
SERVES 20

The EYE AND EAR ALERT project was established in 1968. The Junior League successfully screens approximately one thousand children per year for early detection of eye and ear problems. When problems are detected, parents are notified and urged to seek medical follow-up. League volunteers are trained to perform the screenings at various schools and churches throughout Palm Beach County. In 2002, Eye and Ear Alert went mobile four times and continues to be a successful program for the League.

WORTH TASTING

COOL CUCUMBER DIP

2   large cucumbers, finely grated
1/2   cup vinegar
1   tablespoon salt
16   ounces cream cheese, softened
3/4   cup mayonnaise
1/2   teaspoon garlic salt

Combine the cucumbers, vinegar and salt in a bowl and mix well. Chill, covered, for 8 to 10 hours. Drain and press the excess moisture from the cucumbers.

Combine the cucumbers, cream cheese, mayonnaise and garlic salt in a bowl and mix well. Serve with butter crackers.

SERVES 24

CREAMY YOGURT FRUIT DIP

8   ounces light cream cheese
6   ounces orange yogurt
1/2   cup orange marmalade
1/8   teaspoon ground nutmeg
2   tablespoons coarsely chopped pecans
Shredded orange zest to taste
Nutmeg to taste
Chopped fresh fruit

Beat the cream cheese in a mixing bowl at medium speed until creamy. Add the yogurt, marmalade and 1/8 teaspoon nutmeg and beat until smooth. Spoon the cream cheese mixture into a serving bowl and sprinkle with the pecans, orange zest and nutmeg to taste.

Serve with assorted fruit such as apple slices, pear slices, cantaloupe chunks, honeydew melon chunks, strawberries and/or pineapple chunks. If desired, chill, covered, for 30 minutes before serving to allow the flavors to blend.

SERVES 20

WORTH TASTING

BUFFALO CHICKEN WING DIP

8	ounces cream cheese, softened	1	(16-ounce) bottle blue cheese
4	cups shredded cooked chicken		salad dressing
1	(12-ounce) bottle Buffalo wing sauce	8	ounces mozzarella cheese, shredded

Spread the cream cheese over the bottom of a shallow 2-quart baking dish. Mix the chicken and sauce in a bowl and spread the chicken mixture over the cream cheese. Drizzle with the salad dressing and sprinkle with the cheese.

Bake at 350 degrees for 30 minutes. Broil at the end of the baking process for the desired look. Serve warm with tortilla chips and celery sticks. A boneless nonfried version of a favorite dish.

SERVES 24 OR MORE

The recipe for BUFFALO CHICKEN WINGS *was created one evening in 1962 by Teressa and Frank Bellissimo, the owners of the Anchor Bar in Buffalo, New York. Their son came home late and hungry with a bunch of friends so Teressa began to put some snacks together with whatever she could find in the Bar's kitchen. Frank tells the story that he had a delivery of wings instead of backs and Teressa improvised and came up with the famous dish. July 29th has since been proclaimed the official "Chicken Wing Day" by the city of Buffalo.*

ROASTED RED PEPPER, CORN AND BLACK BEAN SALSA

2	(15-ounce) cans black beans, drained and rinsed	3	green onions, sliced
		1	large red bell pepper
1	(15-ounce) can corn, drained and rinsed	6	to 8 ounces canned tomato juice
1 1/2	cups hot thick salsa	1/2	cup minced fresh cilantro
		Salt to taste	

Combine the beans, corn, salsa and green onions in a bowl and mix well. Place the bell pepper on a baking sheet and broil until the skin is blistered and charred, turning frequently. Remove the bell pepper to a glass bowl and let stand, covered, until cool. Peel and seed the bell pepper. Chop into 1/2-inch pieces.

Add the roasted bell pepper and tomato juice to the bean mixture and mix well. Stir in the cilantro. Chill, covered, for 1 hour or for up to 2 days. Stir and season with salt. Serve with tortilla chips.

MAKES 6 CUPS

WORTH TASTING

CAROLINA CAVIAR

2	(15-ounce) cans black beans, drained and rinsed
1	(15-ounce) can gold and white corn, drained and rinsed
1	red bell pepper, chopped
3/4	cup chopped red onion
1/2	cup balsamic vinegar, or to taste
1/3	cup olive oil, or to taste
1/4	cup cilantro, chopped
2	large fresh jalapeño chiles, chopped, or to taste
1	tablespoon spicy mustard

Combine the beans, corn, bell pepper, onion, vinegar, olive oil, cilantro, jalapeño chiles and spicy mustard in a large serving bowl and mix well. Chill, covered, for 1 hour or for up to 3 days. Serve with tortilla chips. You may serve immediately, but the flavor is enhanced if chilled before serving.

SERVES 20

Brush up on your CAVIAR *terminology.*

BELUGA: *These large eggs come from the beluga sturgeon and are considered the highest-quality caviar.*

OSETRA and SEVRUGA: *These smaller eggs come from a smaller sturgeon and are of high quality.*

MALOSSOL: *The word means "lightly salted" and can refer to beluga, osetra, or sevruga.*

SALMON: *These red eggs from Alaska are of excellent quality.*

WHITEFISH: *These golden-colored eggs from the Great Lakes lack taste.*

LUMPFISH: *These hard, lesser quality eggs are loaded with black dye.*

WORTH TASTING

CAJUN CREAM CHEESE

1/2	(10-ounce) jar apple jelly	1/4	cup dark mustard
1/2	(10-ounce) jar pineapple preserves	1/2	teaspoon pepper
1/4	cup prepared horseradish	1	(8-ounce) block cream cheese

Combine the jelly, preserves, horseradish, dark mustard and pepper in a bowl and mix well. Spoon the jelly mixture over the cream cheese on a platter. Serve with Wheat Thins.

SERVES 8

UPTOWN FROMAGE

16	ounces cream cheese	1/2	cup oil-pack sun-dried tomatoes,
8	ounces goat cheese		drained and chopped
2	garlic cloves, minced	1/4	cup pine nuts
1 1/2	tablespoons chopped fresh oregano	2	baguettes, thinly sliced
1/4	cup basil pesto		

Line a loaf pan with plastic wrap; tape is helpful in keeping the plastic wrap in place. Combine the cream cheese, goat cheese, garlic and oregano in a food processor and process until blended. Spread one-third of the cheese mixture over the bottom of the prepared loaf pan. Top with the pesto and spread with half the remaining cheese mixture. Sprinkle with the tomatoes and spread with the remaining cheese mixture.

Chill, covered, for 8 hours or longer. Invert the pan onto a serving plate and discard the plastic wrap. Sprinkle the top of the cheese loaf with the pine nuts, pressing lightly to ensure the pine nuts adhere. Garnish with sprigs of oregano. Serve with the baguette slices. Do not substitute feta cheese for the goat cheese.

SERVES 12 TO 16

FETA CHEESE *derives its name from the country of origin, Greece.*
Feta cheese can be made from sheep's, goat's, or cow's milk.
It is preserved in brine or oil and is very salty. To reduce the salty flavor,
soak in cold water or milk for a few minutes and drain before using.

WORTH TASTING

ON-THE-GO APPETIZER

1   (8-ounce) block cream cheese
1   (7-ounce) container pesto
1   (3-ounce) package sun-dried tomatoes, chopped (optional)

Arrange the cream cheese on a serving platter. Mix the pesto and sun-dried tomatoes in a bowl and spoon the pesto mixture over the cream cheese. Serve with Wheat Thins and/or assorted party crackers.

SERVES 8

KALAMATA OLIVE TAPENADE

25 to 30 kalamata olives
3   to 5 garlic cloves
1   tablespoon (or more) extra-virgin
       olive oil
Freshly ground pepper to taste
Extra-virgin olive oil for brushing
1   loaf crusty Italian bread

Drain the olives and discard the stems and pits. Pulse the garlic in a food processor until finely minced. Add the olives and 1 tablespoon olive oil and pulse until of the consistency of a coarse paste, adding additional olive oil as needed for the desired consistency. Season with pepper.

Wrap the bread loaf in foil and heat in a 350-degree oven for 10 minutes or until warm. Microwave the desired amount of olive oil in a microwave-safe cruet until warm. Cut the bread loaf into thick slices and brush both sides of the slices with the warm olive oil. Top each slice with some of the tapenade. Cut the slices into halves or thirds and arrange on a serving plate. Serve immediately.

SERVES 12

WORTH TASTING

MUSHROOM PUFFS

2	(8-count) cans crescent rolls		2	green onions, chopped
8	ounces cream cheese, softened		1	teaspoon seasoned salt
1	(4-ounce) can mushrooms, drained and chopped		1	egg, beaten
			2	tablespoons poppy seeds

Unroll the crescent roll dough and press the perforations to seal, forming two rectangles. Mix the cream cheese, mushrooms, green onions and seasoned salt in a bowl until combined. Spread the cream cheese mixture evenly over the two rectangles and roll as for a jelly roll to enclose the filling. Cut each roll into 1-inch slices.

Arrange the slices cut side up in a single layer on a baking sheet. Brush with the egg and sprinkle with the poppy seeds. Bake at 375 degrees for 10 minutes. Serve hot. You may freeze for future use.

MAKES 4 DOZEN PUFFS

MUSHROOMS *have recently come into their own and you can now find more than just the typical plain white button mushroom in your local supermarket.*

CREMINI *mushrooms are closely related to white button mushrooms but are firm and brown. They have an earthy flavor. When a cremino mushroom grows to four to six inches in diameter, it is called a portobello mushroom.*

PORCINI *mushrooms come from Italy and are usually sold dried. Reconstitute in hot water.*

SHIITAKE *mushrooms come from Asia and have dark brown meaty caps.*

CHANTERELLE *mushrooms have very frilly, flower-like caps and are yellow in color. They grow in the fall.*

ENOKI *mushrooms come from Japan and do not look like a typical mushroom. They are long and thin with little caps. Enoki do not have much flavor and are used for garnishes.*

MOREL *mushrooms are considered the "king" of the mushrooms. They have a thick stem, bulky cap, and are expensive, but delicious.*

CHEDDAR DATES

2 cups (8 ounces) shredded sharp Cheddar cheese	1/2 cup (1 stick) butter, melted
1 1/4 cups all-purpose flour	24 pitted dates
2 tablespoons chopped fresh rosemary	24 pecan halves, toasted
1 teaspoon salt	1 egg white, lightly beaten
	1/4 teaspoon sugar

Combine the cheese, flour, rosemary and salt in a bowl and mix well. Add the butter and stir just until moistened; the dough will be lumpy. Knead until the oil from the butter softens the dough.

Make a lengthwise slit in each date and stuff each date with one pecan half. Press 1 generous tablespoon of the dough around each date, covering completely. Chill, covered, for 45 minutes, or freeze for up to 1 month.

Arrange the dates in a single layer on a greased baking sheet. Brush with the egg white and sprinkle with the sugar. Bake at 350 degrees for 25 minutes. Remove the dates to a wire rack. Serve warm or at room temperature.

MAKES 24 TO 30 DATES

DOUBLE CHEESE MEATBALLS

2 pounds lean ground beef	2 eggs, lightly beaten
2 pounds ground pork	1 tablespoon Italian seasoning
1 onion, minced	1 tablespoon kosher salt
1/2 cup chopped fresh parsley	1 1/2 cups (6 ounces) grated Parmesan cheese
1/4 cup olive oil	
2 slices sourdough bread, torn into pieces	1 tablespoon freshly ground pepper
5 garlic cloves, minced	1 1/2 cups ricotta cheese

Combine the ground beef, ground pork, onion, parsley, olive oil, bread, garlic, eggs, Italian seasoning, salt, 1 cup of the Parmesan cheese and 2 teaspoons of the pepper in a large bowl and mix just until combined. Shape by 3/4-cupfuls into sixteen to eighteen meatballs. Arrange the meatballs in a single layer in a baking pan.

Place the baking pan on an oven rack in the upper third of the oven. Bake at 400 degrees for 20 minutes. Remove from the oven. Mix the remaining 1/2 cup Parmesan cheese, remaining 1 teaspoon pepper and the ricotta cheese in a bowl. Spoon about 1 tablespoon of the cheese mixture on each meatball. Broil for 3 to 5 minutes or until the cheese mixture begins to brown. You may freeze for future use.

MAKES 16 TO 18 MEATBALLS

CURRIED CHICKEN SKEWERS

2   whole chicken breasts, split, skinned and boned

2   cups half-and-half

1¹/₂ cups mayonnaise

3   tablespoons mango chutney

2   tablespoons dry sherry

1   tablespoon sherry vinegar or apple cider vinegar

2   tablespoons plus 1 teaspoon curry powder

1   teaspoon turmeric

2   cups salted peanuts, finely chopped

Arrange the chicken in a shallow baking dish. Pour the half-and-half over the chicken and bake at 350 degrees for 30 minutes. Let stand until cool. Combine the mayonnaise, chutney, sherry, vinegar, curry powder and turmeric in a blender and process until blended.

Cut the chicken into 1-inch pieces and thread the chicken pieces individually on wooden skewers. Dip the chicken in the chutney mixture and coat with the peanuts. Chill, covered, for 30 minutes or longer before serving.

SERVES 20

The FIRST UNITED METHODIST CHURCH *building stood empty*
for nine years, yet during this time it remained a meeting place. A local West Palm Beach
resident established a program for feeding the homeless, who assembled outside
the building. Local churches, youth groups, and school service clubs helped expand the outreach
to include regular Tuesday evening meals, Sunday morning breakfast, and holiday
celebrations. Once remodeled as the Harret Himmel Theater, the original church building
again encouraged people to gather for food and fellowship.

WORTH TASTING

PAN-SEARED FLORIDA CRAB CAKES

1	pound crab meat, drained and flaked	1/8	teaspoon cayenne pepper
1	egg, lightly beaten		Salt and pepper to taste
1/4	cup minced red bell pepper	2	tablespoons (or less) plain bread crumbs
4	teaspoons mayonnaise		Unbleached all-purpose flour for coating
2	teaspoons prepared mustard		Olive oil for sautéing

Combine the crab meat, egg, bell pepper, mayonnaise, prepared mustard, cayenne pepper, salt and pepper in a bowl and mix gently. Mix in just enough of the bread crumbs to bind the crab meat mixture together. Shape into four cakes and coat with flour.

Heat a small amount of olive oil in a nonstick skillet until hot. Add the crab cakes to the hot oil and cook until golden brown on both sides. Serve warm with tartar sauce.

MAKES 4 CRAB CAKES

CRAB CLAWS COCONUT

24	stone crab claws	1 1/4	cups milk
1 1/2	cups all-purpose flour	1/2	cup all-purpose flour
1 1/2	teaspoons baking powder	2	cups shredded coconut
1	teaspoon curry powder		Canola oil for frying
	Salt to taste	1	cup sweet-and-sour sauce

Rinse the claws and crack open. Remove the shells, leaving the crab meat attached to the main part of the claw. Mix 1 1/2 cups flour, the baking powder, curry powder and salt in a bowl. Add the milk and stir until blended. Pour 1/2 cup flour and the coconut into two shallow dishes. Coat the crab claws with the flour, dip in the batter and then coat with the coconut.

Pour enough canola oil into a large skillet to cover the crab claws. Heat to 350 degrees and add the crab claws. Fry until the coconut is golden brown. Drain on a plate lined with paper towels. Serve warm with the sweet-and-sour sauce.

MAKES 2 DOZEN CLAWS

WORTH TASTING

SHRIMP SEVICHE MARTINI

1   pound shrimp, peeled and deveined

Juice of 6 limes (about)

3   or 4 Roma tomatoes, seeded and chopped

1/2   small yellow onion, chopped

1   jalapeño chile, seeded and finely chopped

1/4   cup chopped cilantro leaves

1/4   teaspoon Mexican oregano

1/16 teaspoon ground cumin

1/16 teaspoon ground Mexican cinnamon

2   avocados, chopped

Place the shrimp in a glass bowl and pour enough lime juice over the shrimp to totally cover. Chill, covered, for 1 hour or until the shrimp turn pink. Remove the shrimp using a slotted spoon, reserving the marinade. Chop the shrimp into bite-size pieces and return to the reserved marinade. Stir in the tomatoes, onion, jalapeño chile, cilantro, oregano, cumin and cinnamon.

Chill, covered, for 1 to 10 hours to allow the flavors to marry. Stir in the avocado. Serve immediately in chilled martini glasses with spoons. Garnish with sprigs of cilantro or lime slices. The Mexican oregano and Mexican cinnamon have stronger flavors and thus enhance the flavor of the seviche. They can be found at Hispanic markets.

SERVES 6

SEVICHE, *or* CEVICHE, *is a manner in which to cook seafood that involves only the acidity of citrus juices and no heat. Seviche comes from Central and South America and there are many varieties. You can prepare it with shellfish or fish and any combination of citrus fruits.*

SHRIMP CONFETTI

1¹/2   pounds large (about 30 shrimp) shrimp,
        cooked, peeled and deveined
1   cup minced onion
1   cup snipped fresh parsley
2/3   cup vegetable oil
1/2   cup red wine vinegar
1   garlic clove, minced
1¹/2   teaspoons salt
1/8   teaspoon pepper

Combine the shrimp, onion and parsley in a large bowl and mix well. Whisk the oil, vinegar, garlic, salt and pepper in a small bowl until combined. Pour the oil mixture over the shrimp mixture and mix until coated. Marinate, covered, for 1 hour or longer, stirring occasionally. Add sliced purple onion and red and green bell pepper rings for color if desired.

MAKES ABOUT 30 SHRIMP

SHRIMP AND BACON WRAPS

2   pounds frozen peeled medium to large shrimp
2   pounds sliced bacon

Thaw the shrimp in a colander in the refrigerator. Wrap one slice of the bacon around each shrimp and secure with wooden picks. Arrange the shrimp on a baking sheet and bake at 350 degrees for 10 to 15 minutes or until the bacon is cooked through. Serve warm with sweet-and-sour sauce. You may substitute scallops for the shrimp.

MAKES 20 TO 25 SERVINGS

WORTH TASTING

KEY LIMEADE

40   (about) Key limes
1   cup sugar
1   cup tap water
1   tablespoon grated orange zest
4   cups bottled or filtered water

Zest the limes. Juice enough of the limes to measure 1 cup juice and reserve. (A hand-held lime press works best for juicing the limes.) Mix the sugar and tap water in a small saucepan with high sides and bring to a boil. Boil for about 5 minutes for a simple syrup. Remove from the heat and carefully add the lime zest and orange zest. Let stand, covered, for 30 minutes for the flavors to infuse.

Combine the bottled water, reserved lime juice and simple syrup in a pitcher and mix well. Pour over ice in glasses and garnish each serving with sprigs of fresh mint or thinly sliced Key limes.

SERVES 4

GREEN TEA CITRUS PUNCH

1   quart brewed green tea, cooled
2   cups orange juice
2^1/2 cups pineapple juice
2   cups ginger ale
5   drops (about) of green food coloring
1   (20-ounce) can crushed pineapple, drained
1/2 pint lime sherbet
1   large lime, thinly sliced
1   small orange, thinly sliced

Combine the green tea, orange juice, pineapple juice and ginger ale in a punch bowl and mix well. Add the food coloring until a desirable shade of green is achieved. Mix in the pineapple and small scoops of the sherbet. Arrange the lime slices and orange slices over the top of the punch. Ladle into punch cups.

The pineapple, lime slices and orange slices may be frozen in a round ice mold to create an attractive display while keeping the punch chilled.

SERVES 10 TO 14

WORTH TASTING

CHAMPAGNE JULEP

6   fresh mint leaves
1   teaspoon confectioners' sugar
1/8   teaspoon Cognac
Chilled Champagne

Muddle the mint, confectioners' sugar and brandy in a deep Champagne saucer. Fill the glass with Champagne and serve immediately.
SERVES 1

PALM BEACH PUNCH

1   apple, sliced
Sections of 1 orange
1   banana, sliced
1   cup pineapple chunks
Sugar to taste
1   (750-milliliter) bottle Champagne, chilled

Combine the apple, orange, banana and pineapple in a large chilled pitcher and sprinkle lightly with sugar. Pour the Champagne over the fruit mixture and serve immediately.
SERVES 6

WORTH TASTING

PRETTY-IN-PINK LEMONADE

2   (12-ounce) cans frozen pink lemonade concentrate

1   (750-milliliter) bottle sparkling wine

1   (2-liter) bottle Sprite

2   pints fresh strawberries, sliced, or

        1 (16-ounce) package frozen strawberries

Fill a punch bowl halfway with ice. Add the lemonade concentrate, wine, soda and strawberries to the punch bowl and mix well. Serve immediately in punch cups.

SERVES 12

MANGO BELLINI WITH LIME TWIST

2   cups sugar

1   cup water

1   (16-ounce) package frozen mangoes, thawed

4   to 6 (750-milliliter) bottles Prosecco or

        other sparkling white wine, chilled

Lime twists

Combine the sugar and water in a large saucepan. Cook over medium-high heat for 5 minutes or until the sugar dissolves, stirring occasionally. Let stand until cool. Process the mangoes and 1/2 cup of the sugar syrup in a blender until smooth. Strain though a fine mesh strainer into a bowl, discarding the solids. Chill, covered, in the refrigerator. Store the remaining sugar syrup in the refrigerator for future use.

For each serving, spoon 2 to 4 tablespoons of the mango purée into a Champagne glass. Fill with the wine and stir to blend. Garnish with lime twists. Serve with room temperature Saint André cheese and water crackers.

Prosecco is a dry Italian sparkling white wine that is simply delicious. However, any good California sparkling white wine can be substituted.

SERVES 12

WORTH TASTING

RASPBERRY MOJITOS

30   to 40 fresh raspberries
16   lime wedges
12   to 16 fresh mint leaves
1/2   cup packed brown sugar
1 1/2   cups raspberry rum
4   cups club soda

Place the raspberries, lime wedges, mint leaves and brown sugar in a large pitcher and muddle until combined. Mix in the rum and club soda. Strain the mojito mixture into ice-filled glasses. Garnish with lime slices and/or additional mint leaves.

SERVES 8

SUNSET SANGRIA

1   (2-liter) bottle Sprite
1   bunch seedless red or green grapes
2   (750-milliliter) bottles inexpensive red wine
1/2   (750-milliliter) bottle peach schnapps
1/2   (1 1/2-liter) bottle apricot nectar
2   cups orange juice
1/2   (1-liter) bottle club soda
3   oranges
3   apples

Make an ice ring by pouring the soda into a ring mold and adding the grapes. Freeze for 8 to 10 hours. Mix the wine, schnapps, nectar, orange juice and club soda in a punch bowl. Cut the oranges and apples into halves or quarters; do not peel. Add the fruit and ice ring to the punch bowl. Ladle the sangria into punch cups.

SERVES 15

WORTH TASTING

CALYPSO PUNCH

$1^1/_2$ ounces peach schnapps

$1^1/_2$ ounces coconut rum

1 ounce pineapple juice

$^1/_2$ ounce mango nectar

$^1/_2$ ounce (about) guava juice

Splash of passion fruit juice

Mix the schnapps and rum in a highball glass. Add the pineapple juice. Add the nectar and guava juice until desirable; remember the guava juice is heavy on flavor. Top off with the passion fruit juice and serve immediately.

SERVES 1

BLOODY MARY SHRIMP SHOOTERS

Vodka

Tomato juice or Bloody Mary mix

1 to 2 tablespoons Worcestershire sauce, or to taste

1 to 2 tablespoons prepared horseradish, or to taste

8 drops of Tabasco sauce, or to taste

Pepper to taste

8 ounces peeled cooked shrimp with tails, butterflied (about 20 shrimp)

Mix 1 part vodka to 4 parts tomato juice in a pitcher. Add the Worcestershire sauce, horseradish, Tabasco sauce and pepper and mix well.

Fill twenty funky and mismatched shot glasses with the Bloody Mary mixture. Place one shrimp in each shot glass and garnish each with a short celery stick. Arrange the shot glasses on a serving platter and serve immediately. You may prepare several hours in advance and store in the refrigerator.

SERVES 20

WORTH TASTING

RED SNAPPER

1 1/2   cups vodka, chilled
2   tablespoons plus 2 teaspoons
       prepared horseradish
2   tablespoons plus 2 teaspoons
       Worcestershire sauce
15   drops of hot red pepper sauce
4   cups tomato juice

Whisk the vodka, horseradish, Worcestershire sauce, hot sauce and tomato juice in a pitcher.
Pour over ice in tall glasses and garnish each with a cherry pepper and/or celery stick.
SERVES 8

EGGNOG

6   egg yolks, at room temperature
1   to 1 1/4 cups whiskey
3/4   cup sugar
1/16   teaspoon salt
2   cups milk
6   egg whites, at room temperature
3   tablespoons sugar
2   cups heavy whipping cream, at room temperature

Beat the egg yolks in a mixing bowl just until thick and pale yellow in color. Add the whiskey,
3/4 cup sugar and the salt and beat until blended. Mix in the milk.

Beat the egg whites in a mixing bowl until soft peaks form. Add 3 tablespoons sugar and beat until
stiff peaks form. Fold the egg whites into the custard. Beat the whipping cream in a mixing bowl until stiff
peaks form and fold into the egg white mixture. Pour into mugs or stemmed goblets.

If you are concerned about using raw eggs, use eggs pasteurized in their shells, which are sold at
some specialty food stores, or use an equivalent amount of pasteurized egg substitute.

SERVES 4

WORTH TASTING

BRUNCH & BREADS

The Breakers Hotel

In 1894 Henry Flagler, Standard Oil Company magnate and railroad tycoon, initiated the development of Palm Beach with the construction of The Royal Poinciana Hotel on Lake Worth. This premier resort immediately became the winter destination for America's wealthiest aristocrats. Following its success, Flagler embarked on the construction of a second hotel on the oceanfront. McDonald and McGuire Builders began construction on the wood structure in 1895, and The Palm Beach Inn was opened for guests in 1896. When guests made reservations, they often requested a room by the breakers to enjoy the ocean views. Thus, in 1901 Flagler doubled the size of the hotel and renamed it The Breakers Hotel.

The four-story building burned on June 9, 1903, during an expansion project. On February 1, 1904, less than a year later, Flagler opened an even larger version of the hotel. The Breakers Hotel received acclaimed reviews. Room rates started at four dollars a day and included three meals. Guests at both of Flagler's hotels could take advantage of The Breakers ocean fishing pier. The pier remained open until its destruction in the 1928 hurricane.

The Breakers suffered further devastation on March 18, 1925, when fire destroyed the entire hotel. Although Flagler had passed away twelve years earlier, the Flagler family continued in his tradition and rebuilt the hotel for the 1926 winter season at the cost of $7 million. The new construction was overseen by New York City-based Turner Construction Company. The Italian Renaissance-style architecture and fire-resistant stucco building was designed after Villa Medici in Rome. Seventy-five Italian artisans painted the two hundred-foot-long entrance lobby, which was modeled after the Great Hall of the Palazzo Carega in Genoa. With the exception of the center medallion motif, The Breakers' Gold Room is a replica of the Thousand Wing ceiling at the Galleria Dell' Academia in Venice. The Circle Dining Room, with intricate hand-painted ceilings and sprawling ocean views, has become renowned for The Breakers' Sunday Brunch.

Since 1990, The Breakers Hotel has invested $225 million in its ongoing renovation and expansion projects. Today the hotel sits on 140 acres, with 560 guest rooms, two championship golf courses, ten tennis courts, four swimming pools, a beach club, a luxury spa, retail shops, and eight restaurants. The Breakers Hotel is listed on the National Register of Historic Places and remains an internationally acclaimed luxury beachfront resort for vacation and business travelers.

Sunday Brunch

MANGO BELLINI WITH LIME TWIST

ELEGANT EGG STRATA

ZUCCHINI MUSHROOM QUICHE

SOUR CREAM COFFEE CAKE

MONKEY BREAD

CRÈME BRÛLÉE FRENCH TOAST

Nonvintage Champagne*

* see page 170

FRUITED BAKED BRIE FOR BRUNCH

1	(8-count) can crescent rolls	1	teaspoon ground cinnamon
1	(8-ounce) round Brie cheese	1	egg, beaten
1/4	cup raisins	3	red and green apples, sliced
2	teaspoons sliced almonds		

Unroll the crescent roll dough. Press three-fourths of the dough into a square on a baking sheet. Reserve the remaining dough for decorative shapes if desired. Place the Brie in the center of the square.

Slice the Brie horizontally into halves. Sprinkle the raisins, almonds and cinnamon over the bottom half and top with the remaining half cut side down. Pull the corners of the dough around the Brie, covering the round totally. Press lightly to ensure it is totally sealed. Brush the dough with the egg.

Cut the reserved dough into desired shapes using small cookie cutters. Arrange in a decorative pattern over the top of the Brie. Bake using the crescent dough can directions until golden brown. Serve warm with the apples and/or your favorite fruit jam.

SERVES 4 TO 6

TEQUESTA TEA SANDWICHES

6	large Florida strawberries	1	loaf white bread, crusts trimmed
8	ounces cream cheese, softened	1	loaf pumpernickel bread,
1	cucumber		crusts trimmed
1 1/2	teaspoons salt		Mayonnaise to taste
1/2	cup white vinegar		Dried dill weed to taste

Slice the strawberries and cut each slice into four pieces. Fold the strawberries into the cream cheese in a bowl. Chill, covered, in the refrigerator. Using a vegetable peeler, create alternating strips of peel and flesh on the cucumber. Slice the cucumber horizontally into halves and scoop out the seeds; thinly slice. Place the cucumber slices in a bowl and sprinkle with the salt. Pour the vinegar over the top. Chill, covered, for 1 hour or longer; drain.

Bring the cream cheese mixture to room temperature. Using desired cookie cutters, cut two to three different shapes out of each slice of bread. Spread the cream cheese mixture evenly on one-fourth of the pumpernickel slices and top with one-fourth of the white bread slices.

Spread the remaining white bread and remaining pumpernickel bread with mayonnaise and sprinkle generously with dill weed. Layer the pumpernickel slices with the cucumbers and top with the remaining white bread slices. Arrange the sandwiches on a platter and serve immediately. Also perfect for a late afternoon snack.

SERVES 12

WORTH TASTING

HOLIDAY BREAKFAST CASSEROLE

4	slices bread, crusts trimmed	2	cups milk
1	pound breakfast sausage		Salt and pepper to taste
1	cup (4 ounces) shredded mild cheese		Chopped fresh parsley
6	eggs		

Cut the bread into triangles and arrange over the bottom of a greased 9×13-inch baking pan. Brown the sausage in a skillet, stirring until crumbly; drain. Sprinkle the sausage over the bread and top with the cheese.

Beat the eggs, milk, salt and pepper in a mixing bowl until blended. Pour the egg mixture over the prepared layers and sprinkle with parsley. Chill, covered, for 8 to 10 hours. Bake at 350 degrees for 35 to 40 minutes or until set.

SERVES 6 TO 8

ELEGANT EGG STRATA

1/4	cup (1/2 stick) butter, melted	1/4	cup snipped fresh chives
8	cups (bite-size pieces) bagels	8	eggs, beaten
	(4 to 6 bagels)	2	cups milk
3	ounces thinly sliced smoked salmon or	1	cup cottage cheese
	lox, finely chopped	1/4	teaspoon pepper
8	ounces Swiss cheese, shredded		

Pour the butter into a shallow 3-quart rectangular baking dish, tilting the dish to ensure even coverage. Spread the bagel pieces over the butter and sprinkle with the salmon, Swiss cheese and chives.

Combine the eggs, milk, cottage cheese and pepper in a bowl and mix well. Pour the egg mixture over the prepared layers and press down lightly with the back of a wooden spoon to moisten all the ingredients. Chill, covered, for 4 to 24 hours.

Bake, uncovered, at 350 degrees for 45 minutes or until set and the edges are puffed and golden brown. Let stand for 10 minutes before serving.

SERVES 12

ZUCCHINI MUSHROOM QUICHE

1	unbaked (9-inch) deep-dish pie shell	1	cup heavy cream
6	slices bacon	1	cup milk
10	thin slices Swiss cheese	4	eggs
2	tablespoons chopped onion	1	tablespoon all-purpose flour
1	small zucchini, thinly sliced	1	teaspoon ground nutmeg
	Mushrooms, thinly sliced		Pepper to taste

Bake the pie shell at 400 degrees for 10 minutes. Fry the bacon in a skillet until brown and crisp; drain. Layer the bacon, cheese, onion, zucchini and mushrooms in the baked pie shell.

Whisk the heavy cream, milk, eggs, flour, nutmeg and pepper in a bowl until blended. Pour the cream mixture over the prepared layers and bake at 400 degrees for 15 minutes. Reduce the oven temperature to 325 degrees and bake for 30 minutes longer or until a knife inserted in the center comes out clean.

SERVES 6

PINEAPPLE CHEESE CASSEROLE

2	(20-ounce) cans juice-pack pineapple chunks	2	cups (8 ounces) shredded cheese
1	cup sugar	3/4	cup (1 1/2 sticks) butter, melted
6	tablespoons all-purpose flour	1	sleeve butter crackers, crushed

Drain the pineapple, reserving 6 tablespoons of the juice. Mix the sugar and flour in a bowl and stir in the reserved pineapple juice. Add the pineapple and cheese and mix well.

Spoon the pineapple mixture into a greased 1 1/2-quart baking dish. Toss the butter and cracker crumbs in a bowl and spread the crumb mixture over the top of the prepared layer. Bake at 350 degrees for 30 minutes.

SERVES 8

WORTH TASTING

CREAM CHEESE BUBBLE

2   (3-ounce) packages cream cheese
2   (10-count) cans refrigerator biscuits
1/2   cup sugar
1   teaspoon ground cinnamon
3   tablespoons butter, melted
1/3   cup chopped pecans

Cut the cream cheese into twenty equal portions and roll each portion into a ball. Separate the biscuits and pat each biscuit into a 3-inch round. Mix the sugar and cinnamon in a bowl.

Place 1 teaspoon of the cinnamon mixture and one cream cheese ball in the center of each biscuit round. Pull the sides together and pinch to seal.

Drizzle the butter over the bottom of a 10-inch bundt pan or tube pan. Sprinkle with the pecans and half of the remaining cinnamon mixture. Layer with half of the cream cheese-stuffed balls seam side up and the remaining cinnamon mixture. Top with the remaining cream cheese-stuffed balls seam side up. Bake at 375 degrees for 20 minutes. Cool in the pan for 5 minutes and invert onto a serving platter.

SERVES 14 TO 16

A favorite from Heart of the Palms.

WORTH TASTING

JAVA CAKE

3 cups all-purpose flour
1 tablespoon baking powder
1 cup sugar
2 tablespoons ground cinnamon
1 cup (2 sticks) butter, softened
2 cups sugar
4 eggs
2 teaspoons vanilla extract
2 cups sour cream
2 teaspoons baking soda

Whisk the flour and baking powder in a bowl. Mix 1 cup sugar and the cinnamon in a bowl. Beat the butter, 2 cups sugar, the eggs and vanilla in a mixing bowl until creamy, scraping the bowl occasionally. Combine the sour cream and baking soda in a bowl and mix well. Add the sour cream mixture to the creamed mixture and beat until blended. Beat in the flour mixture until smooth.

Spoon half of the batter into a greased 9×13-inch cake pan and sprinkle with three-fourths of the cinnamon mixture. Layer with the remaining batter and remaining cinnamon mixture. Swirl with a knife to marbleize. Bake at 350 degrees for 1 hour.

SERVES 20

The winter season visitors enjoy various WARM WEATHER ACTIVITIES *during their vacation in Palm Beach. Such activities include swimming, lying on the beach, boating, fishing, hunting, tennis, croquet, golf, and bicycle riding. Those seeking more leisurely activities could watch alligator wrestling at Alligator Joe's Farm and watch sack races, contests, and games at the covered grandstand at the Royal Poinciana. Many winter residents participate in cards, casino games, and afternoon teas and dances.*

WORTH TASTING

SOUR CREAM COFFEE CAKE

PECAN TOPPING
1   cup pecans, chopped
4   teaspoons sugar
1   teaspoon ground cinnamon

COFFEE CAKE
2   cups all-purpose flour
1   teaspoon baking powder
1/4 teaspoon salt (optional)
1   cup (2 sticks) butter or margarine,
       softened
2   cups sugar
2   eggs
1   cup sour cream
1/2 teaspoon vanilla extract

To prepare the topping, mix the pecans, sugar and cinnamon in a bowl.

To prepare the coffee cake, mix the flour, baking powder and salt together. Beat the butter in a mixing bowl until creamy. Add the sugar and beat until light and fluffy. Add the eggs one at a time, beating well after each addition. Fold in the sour cream and vanilla. Add the flour mixture and mix well.

Spoon one-third of the batter into a greased and floured bundt pan and sprinkle with three-fourths of the topping. Layer with the remaining batter and remaining topping. Bake at 350 degrees for 1 hour or until a wooden pick inserted near the center comes out clean. Cool in the pan for 10 minutes. Invert onto a wire rack to cool completely.

SERVES 12

Sour cream is one of four types of CREAM *produced from the
fatty oils found in milk. Other types of cream are light, heavy, and half-and-half.
Heavy cream is also called whipping cream and is 40 percent butterfat,
5 percent milk, and 55 percent water. Light cream contains half the butterfat and more
water. Sour cream is light cream that has been processed commercially so that
it sours under ideal conditions. Half-and-half is a mixture of light cream and milk.
It is the least fattening of all the creams.*

WORTH TASTING

CINNAMON STREUSEL COFFEE CAKE

CINNAMON STREUSEL

1 cup packed brown sugar

1/4 cup granulated sugar

1 teaspoon ground cinnamon

1 cup chopped nuts

COFFEE CAKE

2 cups all-purpose flour

1 teaspoon baking soda

1 teaspoon baking powder

1/2 teaspoon salt

1 cup (2 sticks) butter, softened

1 cup sugar

2 eggs

1 teaspoon vanilla extract

1 cup sour cream

To prepare the streusel, combine the brown sugar, granulated sugar and cinnamon in a bowl and mix well. Stir in the nuts.

To prepare the coffee cake, mix the flour, baking soda, baking powder and salt together. Beat the butter, sugar, eggs and vanilla in a mixing bowl until creamy. Add the dry ingredients alternately with the sour cream, beating well after each addition. The batter will be thick.

Spread the batter and streusel half at a time in a lightly greased 9×9-inch baking pan or 9-inch baking pan, ending with the streusel. Bake at 325 degrees for 40 minutes or until the coffee cake tests done.

SERVES 8

CINNAMON *was a coveted spice in the Old World, and it was one of the inspirations for Christopher Columbus' voyage to the New World. His voyage was a search for spices to bring back to Europe. Cinnamon was given as a gift to kings. It is said that men are subconsciously more drawn to the smell of cinnamon than women. Cinnamon is also said to give relief to arthritis and to lower triglycerides. In fact, a mixture of one teaspoon cinnamon and four ounces water consumed daily is said to lower triglycerides.*

WORTH TASTING

MONKEY BREAD

3   (10-count) cans refrigerator biscuits
1   cup granulated sugar
4   teaspoons ground cinnamon
3/4 cup (1 1/2 sticks) butter
1/2 cup packed light brown sugar

Cut the biscuits into quarters. Mix the granulated sugar and cinnamon in a large sealable plastic bag. Add the biscuit quarters to the sugar mixture and seal tightly. Shake until coated. Arrange the coated biscuit quarters in a bundt pan sprayed with nonstick cooking spray.

Heat the butter and brown sugar in a saucepan until the brown sugar dissolves, stirring occasionally. Or, microwave in a microwave-safe bowl. Pour the brown sugar mixture over the prepared layers and bake at 350 degrees for 30 minutes. Invert onto a serving platter.

SERVES 10 TO 12

MONKEY BREAD *derives its name from the way in which one consumes
the bread. It is a pull-apart bread that is baked in a cluster and
one pulls apart the pieces to eat it, much like monkeys pull on everything.
There are many variations of Monkey Bread as you can add raisins,
nuts, blueberries, and/or currants, or make it savory and add garlic, herbs, and/or
Parmesan cheese. The traditional Monkey Bread is the one that appears
in this cookbook and has been popular in American cookbooks since the 1950s.
Nancy Reagan popularized this delicious bread when she served
it at the White House, stating it was President Reagan's favorite bread.*

WORTH TASTING

PUMPKIN SCONES WITH CRANBERRY BUTTER

CRANBERRY BUTTER

2 tablespoons dried cranberries

1/2 cup boiling water

1/2 cup (1 stick) butter or margarine,
    softened

3 tablespoons confectioners' sugar

PUMPKIN SCONES

2 1/4 cups all-purpose flour

1/4 cup packed brown sugar

2 teaspoons baking powder

1 tablespoon pumpkin pie spice

1/4 teaspoon baking soda

1/4 teaspoon salt

1/2 cup (1 stick) butter or
    margarine, chilled

1/2 cup canned pumpkin

1/3 cup milk

1 egg, beaten

To prepare the butter, combine the cranberries and boiling water in a heatproof bowl. Let stand
for 10 minutes. Drain and finely chop the cranberries. Mix the butter and confectioners' sugar in a bowl
until combined. Fold in the cranberries. Chill, covered, for 1 hour or longer to allow the flavors to blend.
You may substitute dried blueberries for the cranberries if desired.

To prepare the scones, mix the flour, brown sugar, baking powder, pumpkin pie spice, baking soda
and salt in a bowl and mix well. Cut in the butter using a pastry blender until the mixture resembles coarse
crumbs. Make a well in the center of the crumb mixture.

Combine the pumpkin, milk and egg in a bowl and mix well. Add the pumpkin mixture all at once
to the well and stir just until moistened. Turn the dough onto a lightly floured surface. Knead the dough by
folding and pressing gently for ten to twelve strokes or until almost smooth. Pat the dough into an 8-inch
round and cut the round into twelve wedges. Arrange the wedges one inch apart on an ungreased baking
sheet. Brush the tops with additional milk if desired.

Bake at 400 degrees for 12 to 15 minutes or until golden brown. Remove the scones to a wire
rack and cool for 5 minutes. Serve warm with the cranberry butter.

MAKES 1 DOZEN SCONES

The SCONE *originated in Scotland. It is a bread that is
halfway between a cake and a biscuit.*

WORTH TASTING

KEY LIME DANISH

PASTRY

6¼ to 6¾ cups all-purpose flour

½ cup sugar

2 envelopes dry yeast

1½ teaspoons salt

1 cup water

1 cup milk

½ cup (1 stick) butter or margarine

1 egg

KEY LIME FILLING AND ASSEMBLY

8 ounces cream cheese, softened

½ cup granulated sugar

½ teaspoon finely shredded lime zest

2 tablespoons lime juice

½ cup sifted confectioners' sugar

1 teaspoon butter or margarine, melted

1 tablespoon lime juice

To prepare the pastry, combine 2 cups of the flour, the sugar, yeast and salt in a heatproof mixing bowl and mix well. Heat the water, milk and butter in a saucepan until the mixture is warm and the butter is almost melted. Add the butter mixture to the flour mixture. Add the egg and beat for 30 seconds; scrape the side of the bowl. Beat for 3 minutes longer. Stir in as much of the remaining flour as possible.

Turn the dough onto a lightly floured surface. Knead in as much of the remaining flour as needed to make a moderately stiff dough that is smooth and elastic. This process will take about 6 to 8 minutes. Shape the dough into a ball and place in a greased bowl, turning to coat the surface.

Let rise, covered, in a warm place for 1 hour or until doubled in bulk. Punch the dough down and turn onto a lightly floured surface. Divide the dough into two equal portions. Let rest, covered, for 10 minutes.

To prepare the filling, beat the cream cheese, granulated sugar, lime zest and 2 tablespoons lime juice in a mixing bowl until combined.

To assemble, roll each pastry portion into a 9×14-inch rectangle. Spread each pastry half with one-fourth of the filling. Roll up from the long side to enclose the filling and pinch the seams to seal. Cut each roll into twelve slices and arrange the slices cut side up 2 inches apart on a lightly greased baking sheet. Make an indentation in the top of each slice and fill with 1 teaspoon of the remaining filling. Bake at 375 degrees for 18 to 20 minutes or until golden brown. Cool on the baking sheet for 2 minutes.

Mix the confectioners' sugar, butter and 1 tablespoon lime juice in a bowl and drizzle over the warm Danish. Serve warm or reheat before serving. If time is of the essence, substitute two 8-count cans of refrigerator crescent roll dough for the pastry. Seal the perforations and proceed as directed above.

Use Key limes in this recipe when available.

MAKES 2 DOZEN DANISH

A favorite from Slice of Paradise.

WORTH TASTING

HERBED FOCACCIA

2   envelopes dry yeast

2³/4 cups warm water

1   teaspoon honey

2   tablespoons olive oil

6   cups all-purpose flour

5   tablespoons chopped fresh rosemary

2   tablespoons dried oregano

1   tablespoon coarse sea salt

3   garlic cloves, minced

2   tablespoons olive oil

3   tablespoons chopped fresh rosemary

Combine the yeast and 1/4 cup of the warm water in a large bowl and mix well. Stir in the honey. Let stand for 10 minutes or until foamy. Add the remaining 2¹/2 cups warm water and 2 tablespoons olive oil to the yeast mixture and mix well. Add the flour 1 cup at a time, stirring until blended after each addition. Stir in 5 tablespoons rosemary, the oregano, salt and garlic. Knead until smooth.

Shape the dough into a ball and place in a bowl lightly coated with additional olive oil, turning to coat the surface. Let rise, covered with plastic wrap, in a warm place for 1 hour. Spread the dough on a lightly oiled baking sheet and punch dimples into the dough with your fingers. Let rise, covered with plastic wrap, for 30 minutes.

Remove the plastic wrap and punch more dimples into the dough. Drizzle with 2 tablespoons olive oil and bake at 425 degrees for 25 to 30 minutes or until golden brown. Sprinkle with 3 tablespoons rosemary and drizzle with additional olive oil if desired. Serve immediately.

This bread smells heavenly when baking. Do not be intimidated by the kneading. The dough is really easy to prepare and is supposed to be uneven and lumpy, so you cannot go wrong.

SERVES 12

YEAST should be dissolved in water that is 105 degrees at the most. If the water is hot, rather than warm, the yeast will spoil. Test on your wrist like a baby's bottle if you do not want to use a thermometer.

WORTH TASTING

LIME-GLAZED COCONUT BANANA BREAD

2	cups all-purpose flour
3/4	teaspoon baking soda
1/2	teaspoon salt
1	cup granulated sugar
1/4	cup (1/2 stick) butter, softened
2	eggs
3	ripe bananas, mashed (1 1/2 to 2 cups)
1/4	cup plain or vanilla low-fat yogurt
1	tablespoon rum extract, or 3 tablespoons dark rum
1/2	teaspoon vanilla extract
1/2	cup flaked sweetened coconut
1/2	cup chopped walnuts
2	tablespoons all-purpose flour
1	tablespoon flaked sweetened coconut
1/2	cup confectioners' sugar
2	tablespoons strained fresh lime juice

Combine 2 cups flour, the baking soda and salt in a bowl and mix well. Combine the granulated sugar and butter in a large mixing bowl and beat until blended. Add the eggs one at a time, mixing until incorporated after each addition. Add the bananas, yogurt and flavorings and beat until smooth. Fold the dry ingredients into the banana mixture with a spatula until almost absorbed. Beat until fully incorporated. Fold in 1/2 cup coconut.

Toss the walnuts and 2 tablespoons flour in a bowl until coated; discard any excess flour. Fold the coated walnuts into the batter. Spoon the batter into a 5x9-inch loaf pan sprayed with nonstick cooking spray and sprinkle with 1 tablespoon coconut. Bake at 350 degrees for 1 hour or until a wooden pick inserted in the center comes out clean. Cool in the pan for 10 minutes. Remove to a wire rack and drizzle the warm loaf with a mixture of the confectioners' sugar and lime juice. Let stand until cool.

SERVES 12 TO 14

WORTH TASTING

PINEAPPLE ZUCCHINI BREAD

3	cups all-purpose flour, sifted
2	teaspoons baking soda
1 1/2	teaspoons ground cinnamon
1	teaspoon salt
1/4	teaspoon baking powder
2	cups sugar
1	cup vegetable oil
3	eggs
2	teaspoons vanilla extract
2	cups shredded zucchini
1	(8-ounce) can juice-pack crushed pineapple, drained
1	cup raisins or currants (optional)
1	cup chopped walnuts (optional)

Mix the flour, baking soda, cinnamon, salt and baking powder in a bowl. Combine the sugar, oil, eggs and vanilla in a mixing bowl and beat until thickened, scraping the bowl occasionally. Add the flour mixture and mix well. Stir in the zucchini, pineapple, raisins and walnuts.

Spoon the batter into two greased 5x9-inch loaf pans. Bake at 350 degrees for 1 hour or until a knife inserted in the center comes out clean. Cool in the pans for 10 minutes. Remove the loaves to a wire rack to cool completely. Use less sugar to create more of a bread than cake consistency. Omit the currants and walnuts for a savory bread. Or, bake in muffin cups; makes 25 to 30 muffins.

Currants can be found in the dried fruit section near the raisins in most grocery stores and in the produce section by the nuts and dried fruits.

SERVES 10

WORTH TASTING

PUMPKIN-CHOCOLATE CHIP MUFFINS

1/2   cup sliced almonds

1 2/3   cups all-purpose flour

1   cup sugar

1   tablespoon pumpkin pie spice

1   teaspoon baking soda

1/2   teaspoon baking powder

1/4   teaspoon salt

1   cup canned pumpkin

1/2   cup (1 stick) butter, melted

2   eggs

1   cup (6 ounces) chocolate chips

Spread the almonds in a single layer on a baking sheet. Toast at 350 degrees for 5 minutes or until light brown. Remove to a plate to cool. Maintain the oven temperature.

Mix the flour, sugar, pumpkin pie spice, baking soda, baking powder and salt in a bowl. Whisk the pumpkin, butter and eggs in a bowl until blended. Stir in the chocolate chips and almonds. Fold into the flour mixture just until moistened; do not overmix.

Fill twelve greased or paper-lined muffin cups with the batter and bake for 20 to 25 minutes or until the muffins test done. The muffins will appear slightly underdone when removed from the oven. Cool in the pans for several minutes and remove to a wire rack to cool completely.

MAKES 1 DOZEN MUFFINS

Make your own PUMPKIN PIE SPICE *by mixing 2 tablespoons ground cinnamon, 2 teaspoons ground nutmeg, 2 teaspoons ground ginger, and 1 1/2 teaspoons ground allspice.*

WORTH TASTING

CRÈME BRÛLÉE FRENCH TOAST

1   cup packed brown sugar

1/2   cup (1 stick) butter

2   tablespoons corn syrup

1   loaf French bread, thickly sliced

1 1/2   cups half-and-half

5   eggs

1   teaspoon vanilla extract

1   teaspoon Kahlúa or Grand Marnier

1/4   teaspoon salt

Combine the brown sugar, butter and corn syrup in a small saucepan and simmer until of a syrupy consistency, stirring occasionally. Pour the syrup mixture into a 9×13-inch baking pan that has been coated with nonstick cooking spray. Arrange the bread slices over the syrup.

Whisk the half-and-half, eggs, vanilla, liqueur and salt in a bowl until blended and pour over the bread. Chill, covered, for 8 to 10 hours. Bring to room temperature and bake at 350 degrees for 45 minutes. Cut into squares and serve immediately with maple syrup and additional butter.

SERVES 6 TO 8

In April of 1999 the Junior League partnered with Wachovia to sponsor the
WACHOVIA WOMAN VOLUNTEER OF THE YEAR AWARD LUNCHEON,
held at The Breakers. The Award Luncheon recognizes women that have displayed
extraordinary volunteer services throughout the year. They are nominated
by the community and voted on by a panel of judges from charitable organizations in
Palm Beach County. The Wachovia Woman Volunteer of the Year Award
Luncheon is in its eighth year and continues to be a successful fund-raiser for the League.

WORTH TASTING

Worth Avenue and Via Mizner

With its Mediterranean architecture, red barrel tile roofs, manicured landscaping, and hidden-away villas, Worth Avenue has long been Palm Beach's shopping destination. Out of its mere dirt road inception, Worth Avenue grew to become an internationally recognized strip for high-end shopping and dining. Originally, the west end of Worth Avenue was home to Joe's Alligator Farm, a tourist attraction that hosted the spectator sport of alligator wrestling. The 1918 construction of the Touchstone Convalescents' Club, which was converted into the Everglades Club, started the residential and commercial development of Worth Avenue.

The Moorish-Mediterranean style was created by architect Addison Mizner with the financial backing of Paris Singer, heir to the sewing-machine fortune. Consistent to the Everglades Club's architectural design, Mizner extended the then primarily residential street with two Mediterranean vias, Via Mizner in 1923 and Via Parigi in 1925. The cluster of small-scale buildings with loggias and winding pedestrian streets that characterize Via Mizner was inspired by the intimate curving pedestrian-friendly streets Mizner encountered during his studies in Spain. Via Mizner originally housed the retail component of Mizner Industries, which comprised the architect's production companies that manufactured various prefabricated architectural elements. Mizner continued to develop Worth Avenue by creating a collection of buildings architecturally related while maintaining their individuality.

Mizner's buildings focused on utilizing courtyards, balconies, and windows to circulate the tropical breeze. Reminiscent of old Spanish towns, the Gothic arcaded sidewalks diverge to vias, which lead to garden- and fountain-enriched plazas. Expanding Worth Avenue's structure, architect Treanor ad Fatio built the Gucci building and courtyard. The east end of Worth Avenue was extended into the Atlantic Ocean with a 1,095-foot pier. Until it was demolished in 1969, the pier was a popular attraction and beach destination.

Worth Avenue became a popular retail destination when escalating rent prices in 1923 caused shop owners to migrate farther south on the island. During the '20s and '30s , Worth Avenue was considered the fashion capital of Palm Beach. The Everglades Club would host weekly fashion shows that paraded the latest trends down a massive runway.

Today Worth Avenue remains at the forefront of the fashion trends with a host of international designers and private specialty shops. The Avenue is home to more than 250 retailers and restaurants. The architectural integrity and immaculate landscape of this prestigious street is preserved by the Worth Avenue Association, which was formed in 1928 and incorporated in 1961.

Ladies That Lunch

PRETTY-IN-PINK LEMONADE

GAZPACHO

CURRY CHICKEN SALAD OVER
HERBED FOCACCIA

PARADISE FRUIT SALAD

MILLION DOLLAR PIE

Riesling, Mosel-Saar-Ruwer, Germany *

* see page 170

GAZPACHO

1   cucumber, peeled and finely chopped

1   green bell pepper, finely chopped

1   onion, finely chopped

2   garlic cloves, finely chopped

1   tablespoon chopped fresh parsley

1   (28-ounce) can chopped tomatoes

1/2 (46-ounce) jar spicy vegetable juice cocktail

1/2 cup red wine vinegar

2   tablespoons olive oil

Combine the cucumber, bell pepper, onion, garlic and parsley in a large container and mix well. Stir in the tomatoes, vegetable juice cocktail, vinegar and olive oil. Chill, covered, for 2 hours or for up to 3 days. Pour into mugs or ladle into soup bowls. A refreshing "liquid salad" for a hot summer day.

SERVES 6 TO 8

GAZPACHO is a cold uncooked tomato soup originating in the Spanish region of Andalusia. Originally, this soup did not contain tomatoes because tomatoes were not available in Spain. The base of the soup was bread, garlic, oil, vinegar, and salt. It was a poor people's food eaten in the fields.

WORTH TASTING

CREAMED ASPARAGUS SOUP

BASIC WHITE SAUCE

$^1/4$ cup ($^1/2$ stick) butter

2 tablespoons all-purpose flour

1 cup milk

Salt and white pepper to taste

SOUP

1 (12-ounce) can asparagus spears

2 cups milk

To prepare the sauce, melt the butter in a saucepan over low heat. Add the flour 1 tablespoon at a time, mixing until the flour is absorbed after each addition. Increase the heat to medium and stir in the milk. Cook for 5 to 10 minutes or until thickened, stirring frequently. Season with salt and white pepper. Remove from the heat.

To prepare the soup, drain the asparagus, reserving the liquid. Chop the asparagus into $^1/2$-inch pieces. Stir the reserved asparagus liquid and 2 cups milk into the sauce. Cook over medium-high heat and stir in the asparagus. Cook just until heated through, stirring frequently. Ladle into soup bowls. For a creamier, thicker consistency, substitute a mixture of 1 cup milk and $^1/3$ cup cream for 2 cups milk.

Substitute leftover asparagus or the woody ends of fresh asparagus spears that normally are discarded for the canned asparagus. Just cut the leftovers or asparagus ends into $^1/2$-inch pieces and combine with enough water to cover plus one inch and simmer for 1 hour. The water will taste like the canned asparagus liquid. Press the ends through a strainer to remove the pulp, discarding the stringy pieces. Proceed as directed above for canned asparagus.

SERVES 4

The BASIC WHITE SAUCE *can also be used as the base for potato soup, tomato soup, hollandaise sauce, macaroni and cheese, and white gravy for biscuits.*

WORTH TASTING

BLACK BEAN AND CHICKEN CHILI

1 1/2 pounds dried black beans
3   tablespoons olive oil
6   boneless skinless chicken breasts, cut into 1-inch pieces
1   yellow bell pepper, chopped
1   red bell pepper, chopped
1   large onion, chopped
6   garlic cloves, minced
1/4   cup chili powder
2   tablespoons ground cumin
1   tablespoon ground coriander
2   teaspoons salt
8   plum tomatoes, cut into 1-inch pieces
1   (12-ounce) can beer
1   cup water
16   ounces sharp Cheddar cheese spread
1   cup chopped fresh parsley
Tabasco sauce to taste

Sort and rinse the beans. Cook using the package directions; drain and rinse. Heat the olive oil in a stockpot or Dutch oven and add the chicken, bell peppers, onion and garlic. Sauté for 10 minutes or until the chicken is almost cooked through. Stir in the chili powder, cumin, coriander and salt and cook for 3 minutes. Add the beans, tomatoes, beer and water and bring to a boil. Reduce the heat and simmer for 30 minutes, stirring frequently.

Reduce the heat to low and stir in the cheese spread and parsley. Cook until the cheese melts. Season with Tabasco sauce. Ladle into chili bowls and garnish with sour cream and additional chopped fresh tomatoes. You may substitute two rinsed and drained 15-ounce cans black beans for the dried black beans and one drained 28-ounce can chopped plum tomatoes for the fresh plum tomatoes.

SERVES 10

A favorite from Slice of Paradise.

WORTH TASTING

SMOKED CORN AND POBLANO SOUP

SMOKED CORN

1/2 cup wood chips

8 unshucked ears (about) of corn

SOUP

4 cups chicken broth

4 cups milk

2 bay leaves

2 tablespoons cumin seeds

1 tablespoon olive oil

4 ounces bacon, finely chopped

2 onions, chopped

4 garlic cloves, minced

1/4 cup all-purpose flour

2 teaspoons salt

2 teaspoons ground cumin

4 poblano chiles, roasted, peeled, seeded and chopped

1 tablespoon chopped fresh parsley

To prepare the corn, soak the wood chips in water for 2 hours; drain. Pull the corn husks back, leaving the husks attached at the base of the cob. Remove the silk and reposition the husks. Tie the ends together with strips of outer husks or kitchen twine. Soak the corn in cold water in a large container for 10 minutes; drain.

Sprinkle the wood chips over hot coals. Arrange the corn on the grill rack and grill for 15 minutes, turning occasionally. Let stand until cool. Cut the corn kernels into a bowl. The corn should measure 4 cups.

To prepare the soup, combine the broth, milk, bay leaves and cumin seeds in a medium saucepan. Bring just to a simmer over low heat; do not boil. Remove from the heat and let stand for 20 minutes to infuse.

Heat the olive oil in a large saucepan or stockpot over medium heat. Add the bacon and cook until crisp and golden brown. Stir in the onions and cook until the onions are tender. Add the garlic and cook for 1 minute. Stir in the flour, salt and ground cumin and cook for 2 minutes, stirring frequently. Stir in the corn and poblano chiles.

Strain the broth mixture through a fine strainer into the corn mixture, discarding the solids. Bring to a simmer over low heat and simmer for 15 minutes, stirring occasionally. Blend the corn mixture using an immersion blender just until the corn begins to break down; the soup should remain chunky. Stir in the parsley and ladle into soup bowls.

SERVES 8

Many words describe SOUP: *broth, consommé, bisque, and chowder. The original soup was called "sop" for the act of dunking bread into broth. Broth, bouillon ("to boil" in French), and consommé are terms for the thin liquid left after boiling fish, meat, poultry, or vegetables. "Potage" is the contents of the soup. Thick and chunky soups are called gumbos and potage. Creamy soups are called bisques. Cold soups are vichyssoise, consommé, and gazpacho.*

WORTH TASTING

POTATO LEEK SOUP

3   slices bacon, chopped
2   quarts (8 cups) water
1   or 2 bunches leeks, rinsed and thinly sliced
5   or 6 potatoes, peeled and chopped
2   or 3 chicken bouillon cubes
Salt and pepper to taste

Cook the bacon in a 3- to 4-quart saucepan until brown and crisp. Stir in the water, leeks, potatoes, bouillon cubes, salt and pepper. Simmer, covered, for 1 to 1½ hours, stirring occasionally. Process the potato mixture in a food processor just until the vegetables are finely chopped. Taste and season with salt and pepper if desired. Ladle into soup bowls.

For a richer, creamier soup add ⅓ cup cream and 2 to 3 tablespoons butter after simmering.
SERVES 4

LEEKS *are a member of the onion family but are milder in taste. To prepare,*
split leeks into halves and rinse thoroughly to remove all the dirt.
You can eat a leek raw or cooked. The cooked leek is ready when the
bulb can be easily pierced with a knife.

WORTH TASTING

BUTTERNUT SQUASH SOUP

2   tablespoons olive oil

2   cups chopped onions

1¹/₂ to 3 teaspoons red pepper flakes

1   teaspoon curry powder

6   cups chopped peeled butternut squash

4   cups water

1   bouillon cube

1   teaspoon salt

1   cup 2% milk

2   tablespoons dry sherry

Heat the olive oil in a Dutch oven over medium heat. Add the onions and cook, covered, for 5 minutes. Stir in the red pepper flakes and curry powder and cook for 2 minutes. Stir in the squash, water, bouillon cube and salt.

Simmer for 30 minutes or until the squash is tender, stirring occasionally. Process the squash mixture in batches in a blender until puréed. Return the purée to the Dutch oven and stir in the 2% milk and sherry. Cook over low heat until heated through, stirring occasionally. Ladle into soup bowls and garnish with fresh parsley. Great start to your Thanksgiving meal.

SERVES 4 TO 6

SQUASH *and* PUMPKINS *belong to the gourd family. Winter squash*
varieties include butternut, turban, acorn, golden nugget, and spaghetti. Summer
squash varieties include chayote, straightneck, crookneck, and zucchini.
The pumpkin is the largest fruit in the gourd family.

WORTH TASTING

TORTELLINI SOUP

1	tablespoon butter
4	garlic cloves, minced
2	(14-ounce) cans clear chicken broth
1	(9-ounce) package cheese tortellini
1/4	cup (1 ounce) grated Parmesan cheese

Salt and pepper to taste

1	(14-ounce) can stewed tomatoes
1/2	bunch spinach, stems removed
1	tablespoon chopped fresh basil, or 1 teaspoon dried basil

Melt the butter in a large saucepan over medium heat. Add the garlic and sauté for 2 minutes. Stir in the broth and tortellini and bring to a boil. Add the cheese and mix well. Season with salt and pepper.

Simmer for 5 minutes, stirring occasionally. Mix in the tomatoes, spinach and basil and simmer for 10 minutes longer. Ladle into soup bowls. Chopped cooked chicken may be added to the soup. If so, add additional broth.

SERVES 4

A favorite from Slice of Paradise.

WORTH TASTING

MIDSUMMER NIGHT'S SALAD

DIJON LEMON DRESSING
2   tablespoons lemon juice
2   tablespoons Dijon mustard
2   tablespoons olive oil
1   tablespoon honey
Salt and pepper to taste

SALAD
4   green onions
4   ripe avocados
8   tablespoon-size slices goat cheese,
        cut into bite-size pieces
Edible flowers

To prepare the dressing, whisk the lemon juice, Dijon mustard, olive oil, honey, salt and pepper in a bowl until blended.

To prepare the salad, trim both ends of the green onions. Slice the green onions lengthwise into strips and place in a small bowl. Set the bowl in a larger bowl filled with ice and freeze for 5 minutes. The cold will cause the green onions to curl.

Cut each avocado into halves and remove the pits. Cut each half into four equal slices and remove the peel. Arrange the avocado slices on a platter and sprinkle with the goat cheese. Add the green onions and edible flowers to the platter. Drizzle with the dressing and serve immediately.

Edible flowers can be purchased from a quality grocery store or you can grow them in your garden. Nasturtiums are an easy accessible choice that are available in a variety of colors. In Palm Beach, they grow well in pots on balconies and patios. Just make sure the flowers have not been treated with chemical pesticides and rinse them well before using.

SERVES 4

Shakespeare coined an expression that comes from Antony and Cleopatra.
*When Cleopatra speaks of her relationship with Julius Caesar, she says
it occurred during her "salad days, when I was green in judgment, cold in blood."
The term "salad days" has come to mean inexperience.*

WORTH TASTING

RED GRAPE AND GOAT CHEESE SALAD

RASPBERRY VINAIGRETTE

1/3 cup olive oil

1/4 cup raspberry vinegar

2 tablespoons chopped shallots

1 tablespoon sugar

3/4 teaspoon salt

SALAD

1 head red leaf lettuce, trimmed and torn into bite-size pieces

1 head green leaf lettuce, trimmed and torn into bite-size pieces

1 (5-ounce) package goat cheese, crumbled and softened

Seedless red grapes, cut into halves

To prepare the vinaigrette, combine the olive oil, vinegar, shallots, sugar and salt in a jar with a tight-fitting lid and seal tightly. Shake to combine. Chill for 8 to 10 hours.

To prepare the salad, toss the lettuce, cheese and grapes in a salad bowl. Add the vinaigrette and mix well.

SERVES 4

GOAT CHEESE *tends to be a bit more expensive than*
cow's cheese because goats do not produce as much milk as cows.
Goat cheese is also called "chèvre" which means "goat"
in French. Goat's milk is better for those who are lactose intolerant.

WORTH TASTING

PALM BEACH PEAR SALAD

2	tablespoons butter, melted
2	tablespoons sugar
2	Bartlett pears, cut into quarters and sliced
3	tablespoons olive oil
1	tablespoon white wine vinegar

Salt and pepper to taste

3	cups arugula
1/4	cup (1 ounce) shaved Parmesan cheese
1/4	cup walnuts, chopped

Mix the butter and sugar in a bowl. Add the pears and toss to coat. Spread the pear slices on a baking sheet and roast at 500 degrees until light brown on both sides, turning occasionally.

Whisk the olive oil, vinegar, salt and pepper in a small bowl. Toss the arugula, pears and olive oil vinaigrette in a salad bowl until coated. Top with the cheese and walnuts and serve immediately.

SERVES 4

PEARS come in many varieties. A Bartlett pear is a summer pear and changes color from green to yellow as it ripens. A red Bartlett is just as its name states—red. Among the winter pears are Anjou and red Anjou, which are egg-shaped, and Bosc pears, which are brown and do not change color. To quickly ripen pears, place them in a brown paper bag and seal tightly. They are ready to eat when they become soft near the stem.

WORTH TASTING

BRIE STRAWBERRY SALAD

SWEET ONION DRESSING

3/4 cup sugar

1/2 cup white vinegar

1 teaspoon dry mustard

1/4 teaspoon salt

1 cup vegetable oil

1 1/2 teaspoons grated sweet onion

CANDIED ALMONDS

1/4 cup (1/2 stick) butter

1/2 cup sugar

1 cup sliced almonds

SALAD

12 ounces romaine hearts, torn into bite-size pieces

1 cup fresh strawberries, cut into quarters

6 to 8 ounces Brie cheese or any other soft cheese, cut into 1-inch cubes

1 1/2 tablespoons poppy seeds

To prepare the dressing, mix the sugar, vinegar, dry mustard and salt in a bowl. Combine the oil and onion in a jar with a tight-fitting lid and seal tightly. Shake vigorously to mix. Gradually add the oil mixture to the vinegar mixture, whisking constantly until incorporated. Chill in the refrigerator; mix before serving.

To prepare the almonds, melt the butter in a saucepan over medium heat. Stir in the sugar. Add the almonds and cook until coated with the butter mixture. Reduce the heat and sauté until the almonds are hard and crisp, stirring frequently and adding additional butter and sugar if needed. Remove from the heat to a platter and let stand until cool. Break into pieces and store in a sealable plastic bag.

To prepare the salad, place the romaine in a salad bowl and top with the strawberries, cheese and almonds. Drizzle with the dressing and toss to coat. Sprinkle with the poppy seeds and serve immediately. You may serve the dressing on the side.

SERVES 4

WORTH TASTING

SPINACH STRAWBERRY SALAD

SESAME POPPY SEED DRESSING
1/2 cup olive oil

1/2 cup sugar

1/4 cup apple cider vinegar

2 tablespoons sesame seeds

1 tablespoon poppy seeds

1 1/2 teaspoons grated onion

1/4 teaspoon Worcestershire sauce

1/4 teaspoon paprika

SALAD
6 ounces baby spinach, stems removed

1 quart strawberries, sliced

To prepare the dressing, whisk the olive oil, sugar, vinegar, sesame seeds, poppy seeds, onion, Worcestershire sauce and paprika in a bowl until combined. The flavor of the dressing is enhanced if prepared 1 to 2 days in advance and stored, covered, in the refrigerator.

To prepare the salad, toss the spinach and strawberries in a salad bowl. Add the dressing and mix well. Serve immediately.

SERVES 6

SPINACH CITRUS SALAD

CREAMY YOGURT DRESSING
1 1/2 cups vanilla yogurt

1/2 cup honey

1/2 cup mayonnaise

1 anchovy fillet, flaked (optional)

1/2 teaspoon minced garlic

1/4 teaspoon low-sodium soy sauce

SALAD
1 large package baby spinach, stems removed

1 (8-ounce) can mandarin oranges, drained

1 (8-ounce) can pineapple chunks, drained

1 cup seedless green grapes

1 cup honey-roasted almonds or walnuts

1/2 cup golden or dark raisins

To prepare the dressing, mix the yogurt, honey, mayonnaise, anchovy, garlic and soy sauce in a bowl.

To prepare the salad, toss the spinach, mandarin oranges, pineapple, grapes, almonds and raisins in a bowl. Add the dressing and mix until lightly coated. Serve as a luncheon entrée, or for supper with chicken or salmon.

SERVES 6 TO 8

PARADISE FRUIT SALAD

1	cup honeydew melon balls	1/4	cup slivered almonds
1	cup chopped peeled peach	1	tablespoon lemon juice
1	cup cantaloupe balls	1	tablespoon orange juice
1	cup strawberries, chopped	1	tablespoon honey

Mix the honeydew melon, peach, cantaloupe, strawberries and almonds in a bowl. Add the lemon juice, orange juice and honey and toss until coated. Chill, covered, for 30 minutes.

SERVES 4

CHINESE CHICKEN SALAD

1/4	cup olive oil		Shredded lettuce
3	tablespoons rice wine vinegar	2	ounces chow mein noodles
2	tablespoons sugar	3	green onions, chopped
1	teaspoon sesame oil	2	tablespoons chopped almonds, toasted
1	teaspoon salt	1	tablespoon sesame seeds, toasted
1/2	teaspoon cracked pepper		
8	ounces cooked chicken breast, shredded (about 3 chicken breasts)		

Whisk the olive oil, vinegar, sugar, sesame oil, salt and pepper in a bowl until combined. Toss the chicken, lettuce and olive oil mixture in a salad bowl until coated. Add the noodles, green onions, almonds and sesame seeds and mix well. Serve immediately.

SERVES 2

The JUNIOR LEAGUE OF THE PALM BEACHES *originated in 1940 with a fifteen-member charter. Its first project was a clothes closet to benefit those in financial need. Over the years, the Junior League has grown their membership to approximately 250 active members. As of 2006, there were nearly 780 active and sustaining members.*

WORTH TASTING

CURRY CHICKEN SALAD

CREAMY HONEY DRESSING

1 to 1¹/4 cups mayonnaise (depends on size of chicken breasts)

1¹/2 tablespoons orange blossom honey

1 teaspoon fresh lemon juice

¹/2 teaspoon curry powder

Salt to taste

SALAD

6 chicken breasts

2 quarts cold water

Celery tops

4 or 5 peppercorns

³/4 cup pecan halves

1 cup (¹/4-inch) slices celery

1¹/2 cups seedless red grapes, cut into halves

Salt to taste

To prepare the dressing, mix the mayonnaise, honey, lemon juice, curry powder and salt in a bowl. Store, covered, in the refrigerator.

To prepare the salad, combine the chicken, cold water, celery tops and peppercorns in a stockpot. Bring to a boil and reduce the heat to low. Simmer, covered, for 45 minutes or until the chicken is cooked through. Spread the pecans in a single layer on a baking sheet and toast at 350 degrees for 10 minutes or until light brown. Remove the pecans to a platter to cool and then break into large pieces.

Drain the chicken, reserving the stock for soups, rice and other dishes if desired. Cool the chicken slightly and chop into bite-size pieces, discarding the skin and bones. Chill the chicken in the refrigerator.

Combine the chilled chicken, pecans, sliced celery and grapes in a large salad bowl and mix well. Add the dressing and toss gently to coat. Season with salt and add additional mayonnaise if the salad appears too dry. Chill, covered, for 3 hours or longer. Serve over Herbed Focaccia on page 49. Or, serve on lettuce-lined plates with hot rolls and butter or butter crackers.

SERVES 8

WORTH TASTING

GRILLED CHICKEN SALAD

BALSAMIC VINAIGRETTE

1/4 cup olive oil

3 tablespoons balsamic vinegar

1 tablespoon dried dill weed

1 garlic clove, minced

1/4 teaspoon freshly ground pepper

1/4 teaspoon dried oregano, crushed

SALAD

4 boneless skinless chicken breasts

8 cups spring salad mix

3/4 cup seedless red grapes,
cut into halves

1/3 cup crumbled goat cheese

1/4 cup pine nuts, toasted

To prepare the vinaigrette, combine the olive oil, vinegar, dill weed, garlic, pepper and oregano in a jar with a tight-fitting lid and seal tightly. Shake to combine. Let stand for 1 hour.

To prepare the salad, grill the chicken over medium-hot coals for 12 to 15 minutes or until cooked through, turning once. Cool slightly. Arrange the salad greens evenly on four salad plates. Top each serving evenly with the grapes, cheese and pine nuts. Slice the chicken and arrange one chicken breast on each salad. Drizzle with the vinaigrette. A light salad with only four hundred calories per serving.

SERVES 4

BAKED SHRIMP AND CRAB SALAD

1 (6-ounce) can crab meat, drained
and flaked

1 (4-ounce) can medium shrimp, drained

1 green bell pepper, chopped

1 onion, chopped

1 cup butter cracker crumbs or
bread crumbs

1 cup finely chopped celery

3/4 cup mayonnaise

1 teaspoon Worcestershire sauce

1/2 teaspoon salt

1/4 teaspoon pepper

Lettuce leaves

Combine the crab meat, shrimp, bell pepper, onion, cracker crumbs and celery in a bowl and mix gently. Fold in the mayonnaise, Worcestershire sauce, salt and pepper. Spoon the crab meat mixture into a buttered baking dish and bake at 350 degrees for 25 to 35 minutes or until heated through. Serve on a bed of lettuce.

SERVES 6 TO 8

WORTH TASTING

PALM BEACH ORZO SALAD

RED WINE VINAIGRETTE
1/3   cup red wine vinegar
1 1/2   teaspoons Dijon mustard
1 1/2   teaspoons sugar
Salt and pepper to taste
2/3   cup olive oil

SALAD
3   cups orzo
Salt to taste
1   red bell pepper, chopped
1   yellow bell pepper, chopped
1   (10-ounce) package frozen peas
1   cup chopped black olives
1   cup golden raisins
1/2   cup chopped red onion
1/2   cup chopped fresh parsley
Pepper to taste

To prepare the vinaigrette, whisk the vinegar, Dijon mustard, sugar, salt and pepper in a bowl until blended. Add the olive oil gradually, whisking constantly until thickened.

To prepare the salad, cook the pasta in boiling salted water in a saucepan for 8 to 10 minutes or until tender. Drain in a colander and rinse with warm water.

Toss the warm pasta and vinaigrette in a bowl until coated. Add the bell peppers, peas, olives, raisins, onion and parsley and mix well. Season with salt and pepper. Serve at room temperature. To save time, chop the vegetables the night before preparation and store, covered, in the refrigerator.

SERVES 10 TO 12

WORTH TASTING

SUMMER BROCCOLI SALAD

1   large bunch broccoli, trimmed and chopped (4 to 5 cups)
1   cup sunflower seeds
1   cup raisins
12   slices bacon, crisp-cooked and crumbled
1   red onion, chopped
Shredded Cheddar cheese
1   cup mayonnaise
1/2 cup sugar
2   tablespoons vinegar

Toss the broccoli, sunflower seeds, raisins, bacon, onion and cheese in a salad bowl. Combine the mayonnaise, sugar and vinegar in a bowl and mix well. Add the dressing to the broccoli mixture and mix until coated. Chill, covered, for 2 to 4 hours.

To save time, premeasure all the ingredients one day in advance and store in separate containers in the refrigerator. Combine all the ingredients on the morning of service and chill until serving time.

SERVES 8

During the 1920s and the 1930s, Worth Avenue traffic centered on the
LADIES THAT LUNCHED. *The Everglades Club hosted weekly luncheon fashion*
shows which featured the latest in trends from Paris and New York. The ladies
who attended the weekly lunch would spend the remainder of the afternoon shopping
for the runway goods. In most cases house accounts were established so that
the stores could deliver the purchased goods to the house and the bills to the estate's
private accountant before the ladies would even return from lunch.

WORTH TASTING

ORIENTAL SLAW

ORIENTAL VINAIGRETTE
3/4 cup vegetable oil
1/2 cup sugar
1/3 cup white wine vinegar
2 (3-ounce) packages oriental-flavored
   ramen noodles with seasoning
   packets

SLAW
1 cup sliced almonds
1 package broccoli slaw
1 red bell pepper, chopped
2 or 3 scallions, chopped
1 cup sunflower seeds

To prepare the vinaigrette, whisk the oil, sugar, vinegar and noodle seasoning in a bowl until combined, reserving the noodles.

To prepare the slaw, spread the almonds in a single layer on a baking sheet. Toast at 250 degrees for 2 minutes. Remove to a plate to cool. Place the reserved noodles in a sealable plastic bag. Seal tightly and coarsely break. Toss the almonds, noodles, broccoli slaw, bell pepper, scallions and sunflower seeds in a salad bowl. Add the vinaigrette and toss to coat.

SERVES 6

SOUTHERN SLAW

3/4 cup vinegar
1/2 cup olive oil
2 tablespoons honey
1 teaspoon dry mustard
1 teaspoon celery seeds

1 (16-ounce) package shredded cabbage
1/2 cup chopped sweet onion
1/3 cup sugar
1/4 teaspoon garlic powder

Mix the vinegar, olive oil, honey, dry mustard and celery seeds in a saucepan. Bring to a boil and remove from the heat. Let stand until cool.

Toss the cabbage, onion, sugar and garlic powder in a bowl. Add the vinegar mixture and mix until coated. Chill, covered, for 6 hours or longer before serving. Easy low-fat coleslaw that goes great with barbecue.

SERVES 10

WORTH TASTING

COOL TOMATO AND CUCUMBER SALAD

2	cucumbers	1	(6-ounce) can pitted black
4	large carrots		olives, drained
8	ounces mozzarella cheese, cubed	1	envelope Italian dressing mix,
8	Roma tomatoes, chopped		prepared

Cut the cucumbers lengthwise into halves and scrape out the seeds using a spoon. Cut each half into thin slices. Peel and thinly slice the carrots.

Place the cheese in a large salad bowl. Add the cucumbers, carrots, tomatoes and olives to the bowl. Add the dressing and toss to coat. Chill, covered, for 3 hours or longer; stir. Serve chilled at your next backyard dinner party.

SERVES 10

GLAZED PECAN DELIGHT

1/2	cup sugar	2	heads red leaf lettuce, trimmed and
3	tablespoons water		torn into bite-size pieces
1	teaspoon salt	8	ounces Gorgonzola cheese, crumbled
1/2	teaspoon cayenne pepper		Raspberry vinaigrette
2	cups pecan halves		

Combine the sugar, water, salt and cayenne pepper in a heavy saucepan. Cook over medium heat until the sugar dissolves, stirring frequently. Increase the heat to high and bring to a boil. Boil for 2 minutes. Add the pecans gradually, stirring constantly. Cook for 1 minute or until the pecans are coated.

Spread the pecan mixture in a single layer on a buttered baking sheet. Bake at 350 degrees for 13 minutes or just until the pecans begin to brown. Remove the pecans to a baking sheet lined with waxed paper and separate the pecans using a fork. Let stand until cool. Toss the pecans, lettuce, cheese and vinaigrette in a bowl until combined.

SERVES 8

Old Wives Tale: Sprinkle a little CAYENNE PEPPER *in your socks to keep your feet warm in cold weather, as many skiers do.*

WORTH TASTING

CANDIED WALNUT AND BLUE CHEESE SALAD

RED WINE VINAIGRETTE

1/2 cup red wine vinegar

1/2 cup olive oil

1/4 cup sugar

1 tablespoon minced garlic

CANDIED WALNUTS

8 ounces walnut halves

1/2 cup sugar

1/4 cup water

2 tablespoons butter

SALAD

Italian lettuce blend

Red seedless grapes

Green apples, chopped

Blue cheese crumbles

To prepare the vinaigrette, combine the vinegar, olive oil, sugar and garlic in a jar with a tight-fitting lid and seal tightly. Shake to mix.

To prepare the walnuts, heat a saucepan and add the walnuts, sugar, water and butter. Cook for 7 minutes or until the sugar dissolves and the walnuts are coated, stirring constantly. Remove to a platter to cool.

To prepare the salad, toss the walnuts, lettuce, grapes, apples and blue cheese in a salad bowl. Add the vinaigrette and mix until coated.

SERVES 4 TO 6

WORTH TASTING

GORGONZOLA, MUSHROOM AND SPINACH SALAD

3 tablespoons red wine vinegar
1 tablespoon olive oil
Coarse salt and ground pepper to taste
5 ounces baby spinach (5 cups)
8 ounces white button mushrooms, stemmed and thinly sliced
1 small red onion, thinly sliced
1/2 red bell pepper, chopped
2 ounces Gorgonzola cheese or other blue cheese, crumbled

Whisk the vinegar and olive oil in a salad bowl until blended. Season with salt and pepper. Add the spinach, mushrooms, onion, bell pepper and cheese to the vinegar mixture and toss to coat. Serve immediately.
SERVES 4

GORGONZOLA, a type of blue cheese, is named for the town in Italy in which the cheese was first made. The term blue cheese is a generic name for creamy cheese made from cow's milk that has veins of Penicillium mold running through it. Folklore says that blue cheese happened by accident when a hapless shepherd discovered that mold had permeated the cheese and ate it anyway. Most blue cheeses are named after historic towns. Some varieties of blue cheese are Stilton (England), Roquefort (France), Danish Blue, Cashel Blue (Ireland) and of course, Gorgonzola.

WORTH TASTING

MARTHA'S VINEYARD SALAD

MAPLE RASPBERRY VINAIGRETTE

1/2 cup raspberry vinegar

1/3 cup vegetable oil

1/3 cup olive oil

1/3 cup maple syrup

2 tablespoons Dijon mustard

2 tablespoons dried tarragon leaves

1/8 teaspoon salt

SALAD

1 head Bibb lettuce, trimmed and torn into bite-size pieces

1/2 head red leaf lettuce, trimmed and torn into bite-size pieces

1/4 cup crumbled blue cheese

12 rings red onion

3 tablespoons pine nuts or chopped walnuts, toasted

To prepare the vinaigrette, whisk the vinegar, vegetable oil, olive oil, syrup, Dijon mustard, tarragon and salt in a bowl until combined. Chill, covered, in the refrigerator. You may also use as a marinade for seafood or poultry.

To prepare the salad, toss the lettuce with the desired amount of the vinaigrette in a bowl. Divide the lettuce mixture evenly among six chilled salad plates. Top each serving evenly with the blue cheese, onion rings and pine nuts.

SERVES 6

WORTH TASTING

CRUNCHY ROMAINE TOSS

1/4 cup (1/2 stick) unsalted butter
1 cup chopped walnuts
1 (3-ounce) package ramen noodles, crumbled (discard seasoning packet)
1 bunch broccoli, trimmed and chopped
1 head romaine, trimmed and torn into bite-size pieces
4 green onions, chopped
1 cup sweet-and-sour salad dressing

Melt the butter in a skillet and stir in the walnuts and noodles. Cook until brown, stirring frequently. Remove to a paper towel to drain.

Combine the noodle mixture, broccoli, romaine and green onions in a bowl and mix well. Add the salad dressing and toss to coat.

SERVES 10 TO 12

Sprinkle SUGAR-COATED WALNUTS *on any salad to give it more flavor and crunch. Combine 1 cup sugar, 1/4 cup water, 1 teaspoon salt, 1 teaspoon ground cinnamon and 1/2 teaspoon vanilla extract in a saucepan and bring to a boil. Boil gently for 5 minutes and add 8 ounces walnuts, stirring until coated. Spread the walnut mixture on a baking sheet and let stand until cool. Break into clumps and store in a sealable plastic bag.*

WORTH TASTING

BEEF, LAMB & PORK

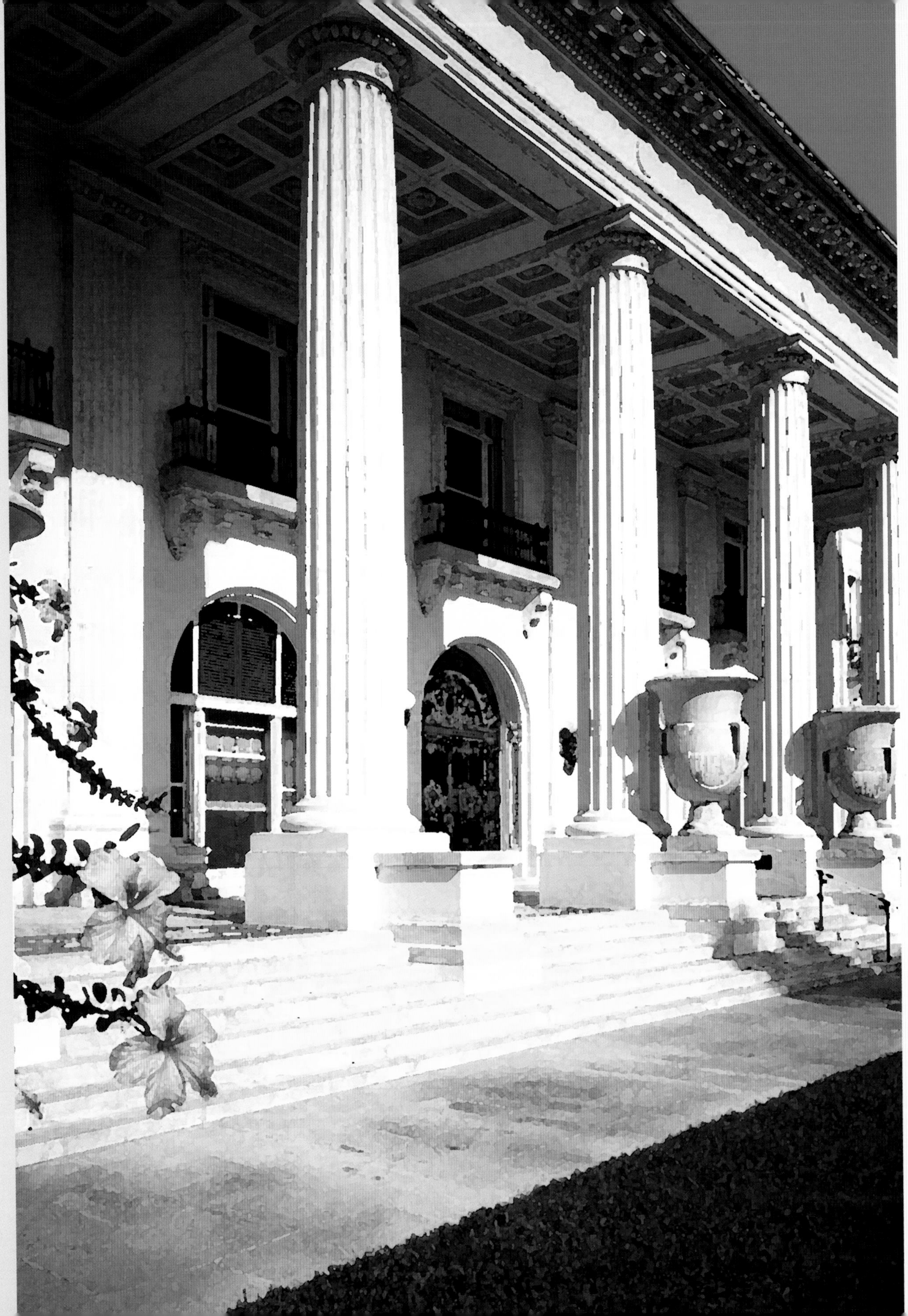

Whitehall

Whitehall was built as a wedding gift for Mary Lily Kenan, the third bride of Standard Oil Company, founding partner, and Florida developer Henry Morrison Flagler. The white marble mansion was the winter retreat for the Gilded Age elite to enjoy the season. The Flaglers would travel south, via Flagler's railroad, to Palm Beach for the winter season and reside there for ten weeks. The official end of the season party was Mary Lily's Bal Poudré, in honor of George Washington's birthday. Whitehall and the Flaglers established Palm Beach as the official winter resort destination for America's wealthiest.

The fifty-five-room and 60,000-square-foot waterfront estate was completed in 1902. Flagler commissioned architects John M. Carrere and Thomas Hastings, both students from the de rigeur Ecole des Beaux-Arts in Paris, to do the project. The Beaux Arts-style mansion facade hosts a white marble column entrance and a red barrel tile roof. A highly decorated wrought iron fence, one of the most impressive fences of its time, surrounds the estate. The mansion is built around the central courtyard, which enables the tropical breeze to circulate throughout the house. The decorating firm of Pottier and Stymus decorated the estate in various periods per room, such as the French Renaissance, Louis XIV, Louis XV, and Louis XVI. The 4,400-square-foot Grand Hall hosts a lowered ceiling to give it the at-home feeling Flagler desired. In addition to extravagant furnishings, Whitehall had the latest technologies, including indoor plumbing, central heating, and electrical lighting.

After Flagler's death in 1913, Mary Lily returned to Whitehall one more time before her death in 1917. The property was inherited by Mary Lily's niece, Louise Clisby Wise Lewis, who then sold the mansion to investors. In 1925, Whitehall was converted into a hotel, and an addition of a ten-story tower was added to the back. The hotel hosted three hundred rooms with the original house used for lobbies, lounges, card rooms, and a bar.

The hotel operated until 1959 and was then intended to be demolished. Whitehall was rescued by Flagler's granddaughter, Jean Flagler Matthews, who established the Henry Morrison Flagler Museum. The mansion was restored to its former state, and many of the original furnishings were returned to the estate. The Henry Morrison Flagler Museum grand opening was celebrated with the "Restoration Ball" on February 6, 1960. The Henry Morrison Flagler Museum is now a National Historical Landmark and remains open to the public today.

Bal Poudré Formal Supper

CHAMPAGNE JULEP

PAN-SEARED FLORIDA CRAB CAKES

PESTO-GOAT CHEESE DIP

CHERRY TOMATO AND OLIVE BRUSCHETTA

CRUNCHY ROMAINE TOSS

RACK OF LAMB WITH MINT APRICOT SAUCE

SAUTÉED BRUSSELS SPROUTS

ROQUEFORT SOUFFLÉ

CHOCOLATE ZABAGLIONE

*Meursault, Burgundy, France **
*Cabernet Sauvignon, Napa, California **

* see page 170

CABERNET BEEF TENDERLOIN WITH SHALLOTS

1/4 cup (1/2 stick) unsalted butter

1/2 cup chopped shallots

1 1/2 teaspoons minced fresh thyme

2 tablespoons all-purpose flour

2 cups cabernet sauvignon or other red wine

1 1/2 cups beef broth

1 cup heavy whipping cream

1 teaspoon tomato paste

Salt and pepper to taste

2 to 2 1/2 pounds beef tenderloin, trimmed

Olive oil for brushing

Coarse salt to taste

Melt the butter in a medium saucepan over medium-high heat. Add the shallots and thyme and sauté for 5 minutes or until the shallots are brown. Stir in the flour and cook for 2 minutes or until the flour browns, stirring frequently. Whisk in the wine and broth and bring to a boil.

Boil for 15 minutes or until the sauce is thick enough to coat the back of a spoon, whisking frequently. Whisk in the cream and tomato paste. Season with salt and pepper. Cook just until heated through. Remove from heat and cover to keep warm. You may prepare up to one day in advance and store, covered, in the refrigerator. Reheat before serving.

Arrange the tenderloin on a rimmed baking sheet and brush the surface with olive oil. Sprinkle with coarse salt and pepper. Roast at 450 degrees for 45 minutes for medium. Remove the tenderloin to a platter and cover loosely with foil. Let stand for 20 minutes. Cut the tenderloin into 1/2-inch-thick slices and serve with the sauce.

SERVES 8

WORTH TASTING

PERFECT PRIME RIB

1   (5-rib) prime rib, bone-in, cut out and tied back on by butcher
3   garlic cloves, slightly crushed
Steak sauce
Montreal steak seasoning

Make small slits in the top of the prime rib and slide the garlic into the slits. Coat with steak sauce and sprinkle lightly with steak seasoning. Wrap the prime rib in plastic wrap and chill for 8 to 10 hours.

Bring the prime rib to room temperature and remove the plastic wrap. Arrange on a roasting rack in a roasting pan. Add water to the roasting pan to prevent the pan juices from burning.

Roast at 450 degrees for 12 to 15 minutes. Reduce the oven temperature to 250 degrees; do not open the oven. Roast for 2¹/₂ hours longer or until a meat thermometer registers 120 degrees for rare. Let stand for 10 minutes before slicing.

SERVES 5 TO 8

---

*In 2001 the Junior League of the Palm Beaches began a mentoring program
at the* NELLE SMITH HOUSE, *a state home for girls ages twelve
to eighteen. The program focuses on self-esteem building and life skills education.
Junior League volunteers provide workshops on topics such as how to
prepare for a job interview, resumé writing, and the proper ways to establish credit.
The girls are also taken on outings to the Palm Beach Opera and Culinary
Institute in an effort to culturally expose them. The League's main objective is to aide
the girls as they prepare to transition into independent living.*

WORTH TASTING

TENDER BEEF BRISKET

1	brisket	2	onions, chopped
Seasoned salt and pepper to taste		2	carrots, chopped
Garlic powder to taste		1	envelope onion soup mix
2	cups red wine	Worcestershire sauce to taste	
1	cup ketchup		

Rub the brisket with seasoned salt, pepper and garlic powder. Arrange the brisket in a 9×13-inch baking pan sprayed with nonstick cooking spray. Add the wine, ketchup, onions, carrots, soup mix and Worcestershire sauce to the pan. Cover with a double thickness of heavy foil and bake at 350 degrees for 4 hours. Serve with mashed potatoes or hot cooked noodles, or serve the brisket on crusty hoagie rolls.

You may prepare the brisket several days in advance and store in the refrigerator. Skim the fat, strain the pan drippings and slice the brisket. Reheat the brisket in the pan drippings before serving.

SERVES 8

SEARED FILET MIGNON

2   filets mignons
Soy sauce to taste
Garlic salt to taste
Butter for searing

Arrange the filets on a dry plate. Pierce both sides of the filets with a fork. Drizzle both sides two to three times with soy sauce and sprinkle with garlic salt. Chill for 5 to 10 minutes; turn the filets.

Heat the desired amount of butter in a skillet over high heat until the butter begins to foam and add the filets. Sear on both sides to seal in the juices. Continue to cook until the desired degree of doneness, adding additional butter if needed and turning frequently. It is very important to keep the filets moist with the soy sauce and butter because of the high heat. Serve immediately with red wine.

SERVES 2

ASIAN-GRILLED FLANK STEAK

1/2 cup soy sauce

2 tablespoons brown sugar

2 tablespoons lemon juice

2 tablespoons vegetable oil

2 tablespoons minced onion

1 large garlic clove, mined

1 teaspoon ground ginger

1/4 teaspoon pepper

1 1/2 pounds flank steak

Combine the soy sauce, brown sugar, lemon juice, oil, onion, garlic, ginger and pepper in a bowl and mix well. Pour the soy sauce mixture over the steak in a dish just large enough to hold the steak, turning to coat. Marinate, covered, in the refrigerator for 6 to 10 hours, turning occasionally. Drain, reserving the marinade.

Arrange the steak on a rack in a broiler pan. Broil 3 inches from the heat source for 5 minutes per side for rare or to the desired degree of doneness. Bring the reserved marinade to a boil in a saucepan and boil for 2 minutes. Cut the steak across the grain into thin slices and serve with the reserved marinade. You may grill over hot coals if desired.

SERVES 4

FLANK STEAK À LA MIMBO

1/2 cup soy sauce

1/2 cup vegetable oil

1 tablespoon liquid smoke

1 teaspoon bottled barbecue sauce

1 teaspoon A.1. Steak Sauce

1/2 garlic clove, crushed

2 flank steaks (4 pounds)

Mix the soy sauce, oil, liquid smoke, barbecue sauce, steak sauce and garlic in a bowl and pour over the steaks in a dish, turning to coat. Marinate, covered, in the refrigerator for several hours, turning several times. Drain, reserving the marinade.

Grill the steaks over hot coals for 4 to 5 minutes per side for rare or to the desired degree of doneness, basting several times with the reserved marinade. Remove the steaks to a platter and let rest for several minutes. Cut across the grain into very thin slices as for London broil. The marinade may also be used for shrimp. An easy and efficient way to marinate food is in a sealable plastic bag.

SERVES 6 TO 8

An old favorite from Palm Beach Entertains.

WORTH TASTING

BEEF STROGANOFF

1½ pounds beef tenderloin,
    (½-inch-thick) boneless top loin
    steak or rib-eye steak
2   tablespoons butter or margarine
1½ cups beef broth
2   tablespoons ketchup
1   teaspoon salt
1   small garlic clove, finely chopped
8   ounces fresh mushrooms, sliced, or
    16 ounces mushrooms, cut into halves
½   cup chopped onion
3   tablespoons all-purpose flour
1   cup sour cream or plain yogurt
Hot cooked noodles or rice

Cut the beef across the grain into ½x1½-inch strips. Melt the butter in a skillet over low heat and add the beef. Cook until brown on both sides, stirring occasionally. Reserve ⅓ cup of the broth and add the remaining broth, the ketchup, salt and garlic to the skillet. Bring to a boil and reduce the heat.

Simmer, covered, for 10 minutes or until the beef is tender. Stir in the mushrooms and onion and simmer, covered, for 5 minutes or until the onion is tender. Combine the reserved broth and flour in a jar with a tight-fitting lid and seal tightly. Shake until blended and gradually stir the flour mixture into the beef mixture.

Bring to a boil, stirring constantly. Boil for 1 minute, stirring constantly. Reduce the heat and stir in the sour cream. Cook just until heated through; do not boil. Serve over hot cooked noodles.

SERVES 6

Mary Lily Kenan Flagler hosted the BAL POUDRÉ *in February 1903 to honor George Washington's birthday. It was the first major social event held at Whitehall. Miniature versions of the legendary hatchet Washington used to chop down the cherry tree were attached to the invitations with red, white, and blue ribbons. All of the ladies wore powdered wigs, hence the name Bal Poudré, which referred to the powdered wigs that were in fashion during the eighteenth century.*

WORTH TASTING

SHERRIED BEEF

2   pounds beef stew meat

1   (10-ounce) can cream of asparagus soup

3/4   cup sherry

1/2   envelope onion soup mix

Salt and pepper to taste

Hot cooked noodles

Combine the beef, asparagus soup, sherry, soup mix, salt and pepper in a bowl and mix well. Spoon the beef mixture into a 1 1/2-quart baking dish sprayed with nonstick cooking spray. Bake, covered, at 325 degrees for 3 hours or 300 degrees for 4 hours or until the beef is tender, adding water as needed for the desired consistency. Serve over hot cooked noodles with crusty French bread and red wine. Quick and easy one-step meal.

SERVES 4

BEEF BURGUNDY

1   pound beef tenderloin or boneless top loin steak, thinly sliced

1   tablespoon olive oil

1   green bell pepper, chopped

Fresh mushrooms, sliced

2   (10-ounce) cans golden mushroom soup

1/4   cup burgundy

Pearl onions

Hot cooked wide egg noodles

Brown the beef in the heated olive oil in a skillet, adding the bell pepper and mushrooms just as the beef begins to brown. Stir in the soup, wine and onions and cook just until bubbly. Reduce the heat to low and cook for 2 hours or spoon into a slow cooker and cook on low for several hours. Serve over hot cooked egg noodles.

SERVES 4

SAUTÉED VEAL SCALOPPINE

12   veal scallops (1/4-inch-thick)
2   to 4 tablespoons butter
1   tablespoon vegetable oil
3   tablespoons minced shallots
1/2   cup dry white wine, dry white
      vermouth or madeira
2/3   cup brown stock or canned
      beef bouillon
1 1/2   teaspoons arrowroot or cornstarch

1   tablespoon water
1 1/2   cups whipping cream
Salt and pepper to taste
2   tablespoons butter
1   tablespoon vegetable oil
8   ounces fresh mushrooms, sliced
Handful of seedless green grapes,
      cut into halves

Pat the scallops dry with paper towels. Heat 2 of the 4 tablespoons of butter and 1 tablespoon oil in a skillet over medium-high heat until the foam almost subsides and add 3 or 4 of the scallops. Sauté for 4 to 5 minutes per side, turning once; the veal is done when it becomes resistant to finger pressure. Remove the scallops to a plate. Repeat the process with the remaining scallops, adding the remaining 2 tablespoons butter as needed.

Drain the skillet, reserving 2 tablespoons of the pan drippings. Add the shallots to the reserved pan drippings and cook over low heat for 1 minute. Add the wine and stock to the shallot mixture and stir with a wooden spoon to dislodge any browned bits from the bottom of the skillet. Bring to a boil and boil until reduced to 1/4 cup.

Mix the arrowroot and water in a small bowl until blended. Add the arrowroot mixture and whipping cream to the reduced shallot mixture and bring to a boil. Boil for several minutes or until the mixture is reduced and slightly thickened, stirring frequently. Remove from the heat and season with salt and pepper.

Heat 2 tablespoons butter and 1 tablespoon oil in a skillet until very hot and add the mushrooms. Sauté for 4 to 5 minutes or until brown. Season with salt and pepper and spoon the mushrooms into the cream mixture. Simmer for 1 minute and remove from the heat.

Sprinkle the scallops with salt and pepper. Add the scallops to the mushroom mixture and mix until coated. Stir in the grapes and simmer, covered, for 4 to 5 minutes or just until the scallops are heated through. Arrange the scallops on a platter and spoon the sauce over the top. Serve immediately.

SERVES 6 TO 8

WORTH TASTING

ROASTED LEG OF LAMB

1	(5- to 6-pound) leg of lamb
1	cup red table wine
1/2	cup orange juice
1/4	cup chili sauce
1/4	cup water
2	tablespoons olive oil
1	tablespoon chili powder
1	tablespoon brown sugar
1	teaspoon cumin seeds, crushed
3/4	teaspoon oregano
2	garlic cloves, minced
1	onion, chopped

Salt and pepper to taste

Place the lamb in a large sealable plastic bag. Combine the wine, orange juice, chili sauce, water, olive oil, chili powder and brown sugar in a bowl and mix well. Stir in the cumin seeds, oregano, garlic, onion, salt and pepper. Pour the wine mixture over the lamb and seal tightly. Turn to coat. Marinate in the refrigerator for 24 hours, turning occasionally.

Place the lamb and marinade in a baking pan and roast at 450 degrees for 15 minutes. Reduce the oven temperature to 350 degrees and roast for 2 1/2 hours longer, basting occasionally with the pan drippings. Stir additional water into the pan drippings for gravy if desired. Serve with Black Opal Shiraz and mint jelly.

SERVES 5

WORTH TASTING

RACK OF LAMB WITH MINT APRICOT SAUCE

MINT APRICOT SAUCE

1/2   cup apricot jam

1/4   cup balsamic vinegar

1/4   cup coarsely chopped fresh mint

LAMB

1/2   cup coarsely chopped fresh herbs (rosemary,
       oregano, thyme and/or parsley)

2   tablespoons minced garlic

2   tablespoons olive oil

2   tablespoons kosher salt

2   tablespoons freshly cracked pepper

2   racks of lamb, frenched

To prepare the sauce, heat the jam in a small saucepan over medium heat until melted. Stir in the vinegar and cook for 3 minutes, stirring frequently. Remove from the heat and stir in the mint.

To prepare the lamb, combine the herbs, garlic, olive oil, salt and pepper in a small bowl and mix well. Rub the herb mixture generously over the surface of the lamb racks. Cover the ends of the bones with foil to prevent burning.

Arrange the lamb fat side up on a grill rack over medium-hot coals. Grill for 15 minutes, or until brown, and turn. Grill for 10 minutes longer for medium-rare. Remove the lamb from the grill, discard the foil and slice between the ribs. Serve with the sauce and Colorful Couscous on page 132. The couscous soaks up the lamb juices and is the perfect complement.

SERVES 2 TO 4

WORTH TASTING

HERB-CRUSTED PORK TENDERLOIN

3/4 cup fine dry bread crumbs

1/3 cup chopped fresh basil, or
    2 tablespoons dried basil

3   tablespoons chopped fresh thyme, or
    1 tablespoon dried thyme

3   tablespoons olive oil

2   teaspoons ground pepper

1   teaspoon salt

1 1/2 pounds pork tenderloin

Combine the bread crumbs, basil, thyme, olive oil, pepper and salt in a bowl and mix well. Moisten the surface of the tenderloins with water and pat the crumb mixture over the surface. Arrange on a lightly greased rack in a baking pan.

Bake at 425 degrees for 30 to 45 minutes or until a meat thermometer inserted in the deepest portion of the tenderloins registers 160 degrees for medium. Let rest for several minutes before slicing.

SERVES 4 TO 6

GRILLED ROSEMARY PORK TENDERLOIN

3   to 4 tablespoons Dijon mustard

3   to 4 tablespoons olive oil

2   or 3 sprigs of rosemary

Juice of 1/2 to 1 lime

2   or 3 garlic cloves, minced

Worcestershire sauce to taste

Soy sauce to taste

2   pounds pork tenderloin

Combine the Dijon mustard, olive oil, rosemary, lime juice, garlic, Worcestershire sauce and soy sauce in a shallow dish and whisk until combined. Cut the tenderloin into 1-inch-thick slices and add to the mustard mixture, turning to coat.

Marinate, covered, in the refrigerator for 2 hours or longer, turning occasionally. Grill for 4 to 5 minutes per side or to the desired degree of doneness.

SERVES 4 TO 6

BARBECUE TOSTADOS WITH
AVOCADO SALSA

AVOCADO SALSA

1   cup chopped tomato

1/2   cup chopped red onion

Leaves of 2 sprigs of cilantro, chopped

1   avocado, chopped (about 3/4 cup), or to taste

1/2   cup chopped seedless cucumber

Juice of 1/2 lime

TOSTADOS

1   cup chopped red onion

1   (16-ounce) package cooked sweet barbecued pork or beef

1 1/4   cups (5 ounces) shredded Cheddar cheese or Cheddar cheese blend

8   corn tostada shells or taco shells

To prepare the salsa, mix the tomatoes and onion in a bowl and stir in the cilantro. Add the avocado and cucumber and mix gently. Stir in the lime juice.

To prepare the tostados, cook the onion in a skillet sprayed with olive oil nonstick cooking spray over medium-high heat for 3 minutes or until light brown. Stir in the barbecue and 1 cup of the cheese. Reduce the heat to low and simmer for 4 to 5 minutes or until heated through, stirring occasionally.

Spoon 1/4 cup of the barbecue mixture into each tostada shell and top with 1/4 cup of the salsa. Sprinkle evenly with the remaining 1/4 cup cheese. Serve immediately.

MAKES 8 TOSTADAS

POULTRY

Mar-a-Lago

The eighteen-acre, ocean-to-lake estate was completed in 1927 for Edward Hutton and Marjorie Merriweather Post, the cereal heiress. Post, who was considered the Queen of Palm Beach, was known for lavish living and generously giving to charities. Mar-a-Lago was the winter home and social center for Post and her many galas, including the Animal Rescue League Benefit Teas, the American Red Cross Balls, and her regular square-dancing parties. The estate not only became a landmark in the social scene in Palm Beach, but an architectural icon to South Florida. Mar-a-Lago was recognized as a National Historic Landmark in 1980 and was the first structure in Palm Beach to be documented and recorded in the archives of the Historic American Building Survey and the Library of Congress.

Architect Marion Sims Wyeth began construction in 1923 on the one million dollar project. In 1925, Post showed off the spectacular estate to Joseph Urban, a Viennese architect, who immediately started suggesting ways to revamp the newly finished house. Urban then spent two and one-half years redesigning and redecorating the first floor of the estate, causing the project to take four years and cost eight million dollars. The fifty-eight bedroom house was remolded to a plush estate with 110,000 square feet, 118 rooms, and over 800 doors and windows. The Spanish-Moorish-style exterior has a coquina and stucco facade. Three shiploads of Dorian stone were brought in from Genoa, Italy, to cover the exterior walls and arches. Cuban barrel tile covered the roof, and the doors and beams were crafted out of Florida Cypress. More than thirty-six thousand Spanish tiles were used throughout the estate, with some dating back to the fifteenth century. Austrian sculptor Franz Barwig and his sons spent almost three years producing the sculptures and relief work for the estate. The living room ceiling is a replica of the Thousand Wing ceiling at the Galleria Dell' Academia in Venice, Italy. The building hosts a seventy-five-foot tower, the largest on Palm Beach. The estate also has such lush amenities as a greenhouse, nine-hole golf course, pool, cottages, cloistered courtyard, and an underground tunnel to the private beach.

After Post's death in 1973, the estate was offered to the nation as a landmark building, but it was refused due to the excessive operating costs. The building stood empty until 1985, when Donald Trump purchased it as a private home. Unable to sell the estate or redevelop the land, Trump's solution was to convert the mansion into a private club. Still today, Mar-a-Lago retains its original design and continues to be the center of entertainment during the season by hosting a number of balls each year.

Alfresco Grill-Out

KEY LIMEADE

SUMMER BROCCOLI SALAD

CURRIED CHICKEN SKEWERS

BARBECUE TOSTADOS WITH AVOCADO SALSA

GRILLED LEMON CHICKEN

COLORFUL COUSCOUS

GUAVA CAKE

*Fiano di Avellino, Campania, Italy**

see page 171

BURGUNDY-GLAZED CHICKEN

1	tablespoon butter
1	tablespoon vegetable oil
1	(2^1/$_2$-pound) chicken, cut up
1	cup burgundy
^{1}/$_3$	cup soy sauce
^{1}/$_3$	cup packed brown sugar
^{1}/$_4$	teaspoon ground ginger
^{1}/$_8$	teaspoon garlic powder
2	tablespoons water
2	teaspoons cornstarch
1	cup sliced mushrooms

Heat the butter and oil in a skillet until the butter melts and add the chicken. Cook until the chicken is brown on all sides. Remove the chicken to a platter, reserving the pan drippings. Stir the wine, soy sauce, brown sugar, ginger and garlic powder into the reserved pan drippings. Add a mixture of the water and cornstarch to the wine mixture and cook until translucent and thickened, stirring frequently.

Return the chicken to the skillet and turn to coat with the wine mixture. Stir in the mushrooms and simmer, covered, for 1 hour or until the chicken is cooked through. Serve with hot cooked rice.

SERVES 4 TO 6

WORTH TASTING

GRILLED LEMON CHICKEN

4   pounds bone-in chicken breasts with skin, or
        favorite chicken pieces

1¹/2 cups lemon juice

3/4 cup water

1/2 cup (1 stick) butter

1/2 cup water

1/2 cup lemon juice

3   lemons

1/2 cup olive oil

1/4 cup (1/2 stick) butter

Place the chicken in a sealable plastic bag. Pour a mixture of 1¹/2 cups lemon juice and ³/4 cup water over the chicken and seal tightly. Turn to coat. Marinate in the refrigerator for 2 hours, turning occasionally.

Melt ¹/2 cup butter in a saucepan over low heat. Stir in ¹/2 cup water and ¹/2 cup lemon juice. Microwave the lemons for 30 seconds for easier release of the juice. Cut the lemons into halves and squeeze the juice into the butter mixture. Cut the ends off three of the lemon halves, discarding the ends and the remaining lemon halves. Cut ¹/4-inch strips of zest from the halves and stir the zest into the lemon juice mixture. Bring to a slow boil and simmer until most of the juice evaporates and the mixture is of a sauce consistency, stirring occasionally. Reserve half the lemon sauce to serve with the cooked chicken. Strain the remaining lemon sauce into a bowl, reserving the lemon zest.

Heat the grill to medium. Using tongs, dip a paper towel in the olive oil until saturated and coat the grill rack using the olive oil-soaked paper towel. Drain the chicken, discarding the marinade. Pat the chicken dry with paper towels.

Microwave ¹/4 cup butter in a microwave-safe bowl until melted. Coat the chicken with the butter and arrange on the prepared grill rack. Brush with some of the remaining lemon sauce and top the chicken with some of the softened lemon zest. Grill until cooked though, turning occasionally and basting frequently with the remaining lemon sauce. Serve with the reserved lemon sauce. You may also bake in a baking pan at 350 degrees for 40 minutes. Omit coating the chicken with ¹/4 cup butter and coat the chicken with the lemon sauce before baking.

SERVES 4

WORTH TASTING

KEY LIME HONEY CHICKEN

4   chicken breasts
1/2 teaspoon garlic salt
1/4 teaspoon pepper
1/2 cup honey
1   cup Key lime juice
1/2 cup mayonnaise
2   tablespoons honey
2   teaspoons Key lime juice
2   green onions, chopped, or chopped fresh cilantro to taste

Rub the surface of the chicken with the garlic salt and pepper and coat with 1/2 cup honey. Arrange the chicken in a single layer in a shallow dish and pour 1 cup lime juice over the top. Pierce the chicken with a fork. Marinate, covered, in the refrigerator for 2 hours, turning occasionally; drain.

Combine the mayonnaise, 2 tablespoons honey, 2 teaspoons lime juice and the green onions in a bowl and mix well. Reserve a portion of the sauce to serve with the chicken. Coat the chicken with some of the remaining sauce and grill over hot coals until cooked through, basting occasionally with the remaining sauce and turning occasionally. Serve with the reserved sauce.

If desired, serve with Cuban-style Yellow Rice. Simply prepare one package of yellow rice using the package directions, substituting olive oil for the butter. Sauté chopped onions and chopped red, yellow and/or green bell peppers in butter or margarine in a skillet over medium heat until very tender. Add the desired amount of frozen peas just before the bell peppers are soft and cook just until the peas are tender. Stir the bell pepper mixture into the rice and serve with the chicken. Spoon the sauce over the rice if desired.

SERVES 4

WORTH TASTING

BALSAMIC CHICKEN

$^1/_2$ cup all-purpose flour

$^1/_2$ teaspoon salt

$^1/_2$ teaspoon pepper

4   boneless skinless chicken breasts

3   tablespoons olive oil

1   large red or yellow onion, thinly sliced

1   cup chicken broth

2   tablespoons balsamic vinegar

1   teaspoon thyme

$^1/_2$ teaspoon salt

$^1/_2$ teaspoon pepper

Mix the flour, $^1/_2$ teaspoon salt and $^1/_2$ teaspoon pepper in a sealable plastic bag. Add the chicken breasts one at a time and seal tightly. Shake to coat. Remove the chicken and shake off any excess flour mixture.

Heat the olive oil in a large skillet over medium-high heat. Add the chicken to the hot oil and sauté for 4 minutes per side or until cooked through and golden brown. Remove to a platter using a slotted spoon, reserving the pan drippings. Cover the chicken to keep warm.

Sauté the onion in the reserved pan drippings until slightly tender and brown. Stir in the broth, vinegar, thyme, $^1/_2$ teaspoon salt and $^1/_2$ teaspoon pepper. Bring to a boil, stirring frequently. Cook for 7 minutes or until the sauce is of a syrupy consistency and the onions are tender. Pour the sauce over the chicken and serve immediately.

SERVES 4

WORTH TASTING

CHICKEN SALTIMBOCCA

4   boneless skinless chicken breasts

Salt and freshly ground pepper to taste

1/3   cup all-purpose flour

1   tablespoon unsalted butter

1   tablespoon extra-virgin olive oil

2   teaspoons chopped fresh sage, or 1 teaspoon dried sage

2   large slices San Daniele prosciutto, cut into 4 equal portions

1   large fresh mozzarella cheese ball, thinly sliced

1   cup pinot grigio or other dry white wine

1   tablespoon unsalted butter

Flatten the chicken between sheets of waxed paper with a meat mallet. Sprinkle lightly with salt and pepper and coat with the flour. Heat 1 tablespoon butter and the olive oil in a heavy sauté pan or skillet over medium-high heat until very hot. Arrange the chicken in the hot butter mixture; do not allow the chicken breasts to touch. Cook for 3 to 4 minutes or until the underside is golden brown. Turn the chicken and cook for 2 to 3 minutes longer or until the chicken feels firm when pressed in the center. Reduce the heat to very low and sprinkle with the sage. Layer each chicken breast with one portion of the prosciutto and equal amounts of the mozzarella cheese slices.

Cook, covered, for 2 minutes or until the cheese melts. Remove the chicken to a platter, reserving the pan drippings. Increase the heat to medium-high and deglaze the pan with the wine, stirring to release any browned bits from the bottom of the pan. Bring to a boil and cook for 3 minutes or until reduced to 1/2 cup. Remove from the heat and whisk in 1 tablespoon butter until blended. Pour the sauce over the chicken and garnish each chicken breast with one fresh sage leaf. It is worth the effort to purchase San Daniele prosciutto and fresh mozzarella cheese from a specialty grocer for the most flavor.

SERVES 4

SAN DANIELE PROSCIUTTO *is a sweet prosciutto with a delicate flavor.*
It is available at specialty grocery stores and Italian markets.

POULTRY

101

WORTH TASTING

MARINATED JERK CHICKEN

1 cup packed brown sugar	1 tablespoon ground allspice
1 cup lime juice	1 tablespoon ground ginger
1 cup fresh thyme	1¹/2 teaspoons ground nutmeg
1 cup fresh cilantro	1¹/2 teaspoons ground cinnamon
1 large onion, cut into wedges	1 to 4 Scotch bonnet chiles
1/2 cup salt	(mild to hot)
1/4 cup pepper	14 (6- to 8-ounce) chicken breasts

Combine the brown sugar, lime juice, thyme, cilantro, onion, salt, pepper, allspice, ginger, nutmeg, cinnamon and Scotch bonnet chile in a food processor or blender. Process until combined. Pour the brown sugar mixture over the chicken in a large shallow container, turning to coat. Marinate, covered, in the refrigerator for 1 hour or longer, turning occasionally; drain.

Cook the chicken in a skillet over low heat for 5 to 6 minutes per side or until cooked through. Or, grill the chicken over medium-high heat until cooked through, occasionally basting with the marinade. You may substitute pork or fish for the chicken.

SERVES 20 TO 24

SCOTCH BONNET CHILES *are bell-shaped with squashed-looking*
pods. They are yellow-green maturing to yellow, orange, or red.
With a smoky apple-cherry and tomato flavor, they are fiery hot and
are available in most grocery stores.

WORTH TASTING

MARGARITA CHICKEN

2/3	cup tequila		1	teaspoon grated lime zest
1/2	cup olive oil		1	teaspoon liquid smoke
1/4	cup fresh lemon juice		1/2	teaspoon salt
1/4	cup fresh lime juice		1/2	teaspoon pepper
2	large garlic cloves, minced		1/4	teaspoon ground ginger
2	tablespoons chopped fresh cilantro		8	boneless skinless chicken breasts
1	teaspoon grated lemon zest			

Combine the tequila, olive oil, lemon juice, lime juice, garlic, cilantro, lemon zest, lime zest, liquid smoke, salt, pepper and ginger in a bowl and mix well. Pour the tequila mixture into a large sealable plastic bag and add the chicken. Seal tightly and turn to coat.

Marinate in the refrigerator for 2 to 10 hours, turning occasionally; drain. Grill the chicken over medium-hot heat for 6 minutes per side or until cooked through. Serve with Spicy Mexi-Cali Dressing on page 139.

SERVES 8

PARMESAN CHICKEN

1/2	cup Dijon mustard		6	boneless skinless chicken breasts
2	teaspoons white wine vinegar		2	English muffins
1	teaspoon salt		1	cup grated Parmesan cheese
1	teaspoon pepper		2	tablespoons butter, melted
1	teaspoon parsley flakes			

Combine the Dijon mustard, vinegar, salt, pepper and parsley flakes in a bowl and mix well. Add the chicken and toss to coat. Process the muffins in a food processor until finely ground. Add the cheese and butter and process until combined.

Coat the chicken with the crumb mixture and arrange in a single layer in a nonstick baking pan or on a baking sheet lined with baking parchment. Bake at 350 degrees for 15 to 20 minutes or until cooked through and golden brown. You may drizzle with olive oil before baking for a nice golden brown color. It is worth the added calories.

SERVES 6

WORTH TASTING

SAUTÉED CHICKEN PORTOBELLO CHASSEUR

BROWN SAUCE

1/4 cup minced shallots

2 tablespoons olive oil

3/4 cup chopped seeded peeled
   red tomato

1/2 garlic clove, minced

1/4 teaspoon chopped fresh basil

1/4 teaspoon chopped fresh tarragon

1/2 cup dry white wine

1/2 cup beef consommé

1 tablespoon water

1 tablespoon cornstarch

Salt and pepper to taste

CHICKEN

3 (8-ounce) boneless skinless
   chicken breasts

2 tablespoons butter

2 portobello mushrooms, stemmed
   and julienned

1 red bell pepper, roasted and julienned

To prepare the sauce, combine the shallots and olive oil in a small saucepan over medium heat. Cook until the shallots start to sizzle and then stir in the tomato, garlic, basil and tarragon. Add the wine and consommé and mix well. Stir in a mixture of the water and cornstarch and bring to a boil. Boil for 4 minutes or until reduced and thickened, stirring frequently. Season with salt and pepper. Reduce the heat to low and cover to keep warm.

To prepare the chicken, pound the chicken between sheets of waxed paper with a meat mallet until flattened. Melt the butter in a skillet over medium heat and add the chicken. Cook until the chicken is light brown and turn. Add the mushrooms and roasted bell pepper to the skillet and continue to cook until the chicken is cooked through, turning frequently.

To serve, spoon 6 tablespoons of the sauce on each of three serving plates. Arrange one chicken breast and an equal portion of the mushroom mixture on each plate. Top with 1/4 cup of the remaining sauce. Serve with rice pilaf, sautéed potatoes or hot cooked pasta.

SERVES 3

STUFFED CHICKEN BREASTS

4   boneless skinless chicken breasts
1   cup crumbled feta cheese
3/4   cup chopped seeded tomato
1/4   cup chopped fresh parsley
1/4   cup fresh lemon juice
3   tablespoons olive oil
1   tablespoon grated lemon zest
1   tablespoon minced garlic
Salt and pepper to taste
Olive oil to taste

Make a pocket in the side of each chicken breast. Combine the feta cheese, tomato, parsley, lemon juice, 3 tablespoons olive oil, the lemon zest, garlic, salt and pepper in a bowl and mix well. Spoon 1/4 cup of the cheese mixture into each pocket. Coat both sides of the chicken breasts with olive oil and sprinkle with salt and pepper.

Arrange the chicken on a greased grill rack and grill over medium-high heat for 10 to 12 minutes per side or until cooked through. To form a perfect pocket in the chicken breasts, use the palm of your hand as a guide and place it on top of the chicken. Insert a boning knife into the thickest portion of the chicken breasts. Slowly saw in and out and then cut the opening just a little bit wider.

SERVES 4

THE JUNIOR LEAGUE THRIFT SHOP *opened in September 1956.*
For fifty years the Thrift Shop thrived on selling fabulous clothes donated by League
members. Originally the shop was run by League volunteers, but as times
progressed and profits soared, the shop became a boutique with a full-time manager
and opened an ebay storefront. In 2006, the boutique was set to sunset.

WORTH TASTING

BLACKENED CHICKEN PASTA

4   slices bacon

2   pounds boneless skinless chicken breasts

Blackening spice to taste

6   tablespoons butter

1   cup sliced fresh mushrooms

3/4 cup heavy cream

1/2 cup (2 ounces) freshly grated Parmesan cheese

1   tablespoon hot red pepper sauce

8   ounces bowtie pasta, cooked and drained

Cook the bacon in a skillet until brown and crisp; drain. Or, microwave in microwave-safe dish. Cool and break the bacon into small pieces.

Sprinkle the chicken with blackening spice. Melt 2 tablespoons of the butter in a large skillet and add the chicken. Cook for 6 to 7 minutes per side or until cooked through. Remove the chicken to a platter to cool, reserving the pan drippings. Cut the chicken into thin bite-size pieces. Melt 1 tablespoon of the remaining butter with the reserved pan drippings and add the mushrooms. Sauté until tender.

Combine the remaining 3 tablespoons butter, the cream, cheese and hot sauce in a saucepan. Cook until blended and slightly thickened, stirring frequently. Stir in the bacon, chicken and mushrooms and cook just until heated through. Spoon the chicken mixture over the pasta on a serving platter and sprinkle with additional Parmesan cheese.

SERVES 4

*Marjorie Merriweather Post served as hostess to Palm Beach's
most extravagant parties. Post is credited with hosting the first charity event,
a tea to benefit the Animal Rescue League. Post established additional
charity events, including the* RED CROSS BALL, *which has become the most
prestigious charity gala in Palm Beach. The most popular party at
Mar-a-Lago was Post's famous square dance. This family affair would include
outside eating, dancing, and socializing. The guest list
would range from influential businessmen to her loyal employees.*

WORTH TASTING

LASAGNA WITH WHITE SAUCE

CHICKEN AND PASTA

3   whole chicken breasts,
        split into halves
1¹/4 cups chicken broth
1   cup water
3   quarts (12 cups) water
1/4 cup vegetable oil
1   tablespoon salt
16 ounces lasagna noodles

WHITE SAUCE AND ASSEMBLY

3/4 cup (1¹/2 sticks) unsalted butter
7¹/2 tablespoons all-purpose flour
2   cups milk

1¹/2 cups whipping cream
1/2 teaspoon rosemary
1/2 teaspoon tarragon
1/2 teaspoon Beau Monde seasoning
1/2 teaspoon salt
1/8 teaspoon ground nutmeg
1¹/2 cups (6 ounces) freshly grated
        Parmesan cheese
4   ounces shredded prosciutto
1   cup chopped fresh parsley

To prepare the chicken, combine the chicken, broth and 1 cup water in a large saucepan and bring to a boil. Reduce the heat and cook for 30 minutes or until tender. Drain, reserving 1 cup of the broth for the sauce. Allow the chicken to cool and cut into bite-size strips, discarding the skin and bones. Bring 3 quarts water to a boil in a stockpot and add the oil and salt. Add the pasta and cook until al dente; drain. Arrange the pasta on paper towels to dry.

To prepare the sauce, melt the butter in a large saucepan. Stir in the flour and cook over medium heat for 3 minutes, stirring constantly. Add the reserved 1 cup broth, the milk and cream and mix well. Cook over low heat until the mixture begins to boil and thicken, whisking constantly. Stir in the rosemary, tarragon, Beau Monde seasoning, salt and nutmeg. Remove from the heat and stir in the cheese.

To assemble, lightly butter a 9×13-inch baking dish. Layer one-fourth of the pasta, one-fourth of the sauce, one-third of the chicken and one-third of the prosciutto in the prepared baking dish. Repeat this process until the baking dish contains four layers of noodles and sauce and three layers of the chicken and prosciutto. Bake at 350 degrees for 20 to 25 minutes or until heated through. Sprinkle with the parsley just before serving.

SERVES 6 TO 8

An old favorite from Palm Beach Entertains.

WORTH TASTING

CHICKEN PESTO PASTA WITH SPINACH

12 to 16 ounces penne	1/2 cup (2 ounces) grated
1 (10-ounce) package frozen	Parmesan cheese
chopped spinach	1 (8-ounce) container refrigerator
1 (10-ounce) package frozen cooked	basil pesto
Italian-flavor chicken	1/2 cup oil-pack sun-dried tomatoes,
(such as Purdue Shortcuts)	drained and chopped

Cook the pasta using the package directions; drain. Place the spinach in a microwave-safe dish and microwave on High for 6 to 7 minutes; drain. Press the excess moisture from the spinach. Cut the chicken into bite-size pieces.

Toss the pasta, spinach, chicken, cheese and pesto in a bowl until combined. Sprinkle with the sun-dried tomatoes. Serve at room temperature or chilled. Omit the chicken to serve as a side dish.

SERVES 6

CHICKEN MARSALA

4 chicken cutlets	1 garlic clove, crushed
1 egg, beaten	1 1/2 cups sliced portobello mushrooms
1 cup all-purpose flour	2 cups marsala, or to taste
2 tablespoons butter	1/4 cup (1/2 stick) butter

Pound the chicken between sheets of waxed paper until flattened. Dip in the egg and coat with the flour. Melt 2 tablespoons butter in a skillet and then stir in the garlic. Cook over low heat until light brown and then stir in the mushrooms and 3/4 cup of the wine. Increase the heat to medium and cook until thickened, stirring frequently. Remove the mushroom mixture to a bowl.

Melt 1/4 cup butter in the same skillet and add the chicken. Cook until light brown on both sides. Add the reserved mushroom mixture and 1 cup of the remaining wine to the skillet and mix well. Cook until heated through, adding the remaining 1/4 cup wine if desired for a thinner consistency. Serve immediately.

SERVES 4

CHICKEN ENCHILADAS

1	cup chopped onion
1¹/2	cups shredded cooked chicken (8 ounces)
1	cup (4 ounces) shredded Cheddar Jack cheese
1	cup picante sauce
¹/2	cup cream cheese
4	ounces sour cream
1	teaspoon ground cumin
8	to 10 (6-inch) flour tortillas
1¹/2	cups green taco sauce
1	cup (4 ounces) shredded Cheddar Jack cheese

Sauté the onion in a nonstick skillet until tender. Stir in the chicken, 1 cup cheese, the picante sauce, cream cheese, sour cream and cumin.

Cook until the cheese melts, stirring frequently. Spoon ¹/3 cup of the mixture onto each tortilla and roll tightly to enclose the filling. Arrange seam side down in a lightly greased 9×13-inch baking dish. Drizzle with the taco sauce and sprinkle with 1 cup cheese. Be generous with the cheese, adding additional if desired. Bake at 350 degrees for 15 minutes.

You may prepare in advance and store, covered, in the refrigerator. Increase the baking time to 30 minutes. To save time, substitute two cans water-pack white chicken breast for the chopped shredded chicken.

SERVES 6 TO 8

WORTH TASTING

SEAFOOD

Sea Gull Cottage

In 1886 R. R. McCormick, a Denver railroad developer, built the McCormick Cottage, the house that became known as Sea Gull Cottage, now the oldest home in Palm Beach. Sea Gull, a substantial shingle-style structure with a third-story cupola, was acknowledged as the "showplace of the lake." With the completion of such an up-to-date home, the end of Palm Beach's pioneer days was signaled.

By 1893, Henry Flagler had purchased McCormick's property for seventy-five thousand dollars. McCormick's house, now Henry Flagler's home, stood at the center of all Palm Beach activities and housed Henry Flagler during the winter months. It was his first Palm Beach home.

The amenities that set Sea Gull Cottage apart from other homes in that era were the "cool, well ventilated rooms, fancy ornamental woods, magnificent mahogany staircase, and floors of marble." The house also contained fancy mirrors, luxurious furnishings, and a cupola, or tower, that lent a wonderful view of the area surroundings. Sea Gull Cottage's architectural design suited Florida well, providing for broad porches, high ceilings, and cupolas. As the finest house in the area, Sea Gull Cottage became the primary design source for the homes in Palm Beach.

Sea Gull Cottage became part of Palm Beach's hotel age when it was moved to the oceanfront in 1913 to be used as a rental cottage to The Breakers Hotel. For seventy years, it served as a seasonal rental for families and their staff during the winter months. In 1983 the Preservation Foundation discovered The Breakers' plan to replace its cottages with new condominiums and began negotiations to save Palm Beach's oldest house. An agreement was reached between The Breakers, the Preservation Foundation, and the Royal Poinciana Chapel, the interdenominational house of worship founded by Flagler, to move Sea Gull Cottage to the Chapel's grounds. The Preservation Foundation agreed to restore Sea Gull Cottage to serve the needs of the Chapel.

Island Party

CALYPSO PUNCH

SPINACH STRAWBERRY SALAD

PARMESAN-CRUSTED GROUPER FINGERS

SAUTÉED FLORIDA LOBSTER AND SHRIMP
IN KEY LIME SAUCE

SUNSET SCALLOPS

ISLAND COCONUT RICE

MARGARITA CHEESECAKE

Albariño, Rias Baixas, Spain*

* see page 171

PARMESAN-CRUSTED GROUPER FINGERS

2   eggs
1   cup (4 ounces) grated Parmesan cheese
1/2 cup Italian-seasoned bread crumbs
4   grouper fillets
1/2 cup (1 stick) butter or butter substitute
1/3 cup lemon juice

Whisk the eggs in a bowl until blended. Mix the cheese and bread crumbs in a shallow dish. Cut each fillet diagonally into three or four strips. Dip each strip in the eggs and coat with the bread crumb mixture.

Melt the butter in a large skillet and stir in the lemon juice. Bring to a simmer over medium-high heat. Add the coated strips to the butter mixture and sauté for 3 to 4 minutes per side or until the strips flake easily; drain. Drizzle the pan drippings over the grouper or serve as a dipping sauce. Serve with hot cooked rice or pasta for a main dish, over mixed salad greens with a vinaigrette for a hearty salad or as an appetizer with dill dip.

For a lighter lemon flavor, reduce the amount of lemon juice. For a crunchier texture, reduce the butter and lemon mixture by one-third to one-half.

SERVES 4 TO 6

WORTH TASTING

PECAN-CRUSTED MAHIMAHI WITH CRAB RELISH

PECAN MEUNIÈRE SAUCE

Juice of 2 lemons

- 1/4 cup Worcestershire sauce
- 1 tablespoon minced shallot
- 2 tablespoons heavy cream
- 1/2 cup (1 stick) butter, chilled and cut into small pieces
- 1/4 cup chopped pecans

CRAB RELISH

- 1 cup coarsely chopped toasted pecans
- 2 tablespoons chopped red bell pepper
- 1 tablespoon minced shallot
- 1 tablespoon chopped green onion
- 1 tablespoon olive oil

Juice of 1 lemon

- 1/2 cup crab meat

Salt and pepper to taste

MAHIMAHI AND ASSEMBLY

- 1 cup coarsely chopped toasted pecans
- 1/2 cup all-purpose flour
- 1 tablespoon Creole seasoning

Salt and pepper to taste

- 1 cup all-purpose flour
- 2 eggs
- 1 tablespoon milk
- 2 (6-ounce) mahimahi fillets
- 2 tablespoons vegetable oil

To prepare the sauce, combine the lemon juice, Worcestershire sauce and shallot in a saucepan and bring to a boil. Boil until the mixture is of a syrupy consistency and thickened. Stir in the cream and cook until the mixture is reduced by half. Reduce the heat to low. Whisk in the butter a few pieces at a time until the sauce begins to lightly emulsify; remove from the heat if the butter melts too quickly. Whisk in the pecans when the butter is fully incorporated. Adjust the seasonings; cover to keep warm.

To prepare the relish, combine the pecans, bell pepper, shallot, green onion, olive oil and lemon juice in a bowl and mix well. Fold in the crab meat and season with salt and pepper.

To prepare the mahimahi, process the pecans, 1/2 cup flour, 1 teaspoon of the Creole seasoning, salt and pepper in a food processor just until smooth but not oily and pour into a shallow dish. Mix 1 cup flour and 1 teaspoon of the remaining Creole seasoning in a shallow dish. Whisk the eggs and milk in a bowl until blended. Sprinkle the fillets with the remaining 1 teaspoon Creole seasoning.

Coat the fillets with the seasoned flour, dip in the egg mixture and then coat with the pecan mixture. Heat the oil in an ovenproof sauté pan until hot and add the coated fillets. Cook until golden brown and turn. Bake at 350 degrees for 12 minutes.

To assemble, cut the fillets into halves. Ladle one-fourth of the sauce on each of four dinner plates and top each with an equal portion of the fish and relish. Garnish with thinly sliced fresh chives.

SERVES 4

JAMAICAN RED SNAPPER

2	tablespoons olive oil	1	bunch scallions, chopped
4	garlic cloves, chopped	1	sprig of thyme
2	cups fish stock, clam stock or shrimp stock	2	pounds red snapper fillets
1	(10-ounce) can tomatoes with green chiles	8	extra-large or jumbo shrimp, peeled and deveined

Heat the olive oil in a sauté pan and add the garlic. Sauté until the garlic is light brown. Stir in the stock, tomatoes, scallions and thyme. Bring to a light boil and add the fillets and shrimp.

Simmer until the shrimp turn pink and the fillets turn white. The shrimp will cook faster than the fillets, so remove the shrimp as soon as they turn pink. Return the shrimp to the sauté pan as soon as the fillets flake easily when tested with a fork. Serve with black beans and rice.

SERVES 4

ROASTED BARBECUE SALMON

1/4	cup orange juice	4	teaspoons chili powder
2	tablespoons fresh lemon juice	2	teaspoons grated lemon zest
4	(6-ounce) salmon fillets	1/2	teaspoon salt
2	tablespoons brown sugar	1/4	teaspoon ground cinnamon

Mix the orange juice and lemon juice in a large sealable plastic bag and add the fillets. Seal tightly and turn to coat. Marinate in the refrigerator for 1 hour, turning once; drain.

Arrange the fillets skin side down in a baking dish sprayed with nonstick cooking spray. Combine the brown sugar, chili powder, lemon zest, salt and cinnamon in a small bowl and mix well. Rub the brown sugar mixture over the top of the fillets. Bake at 400 degrees for 20 to 30 minutes or until the fillets flake easily when tested with a fork. Serve with lemon slices.

SERVES 4

POACHED SALMON WITH GRAPE SALSA

GRAPE SALSA

3/4 cup seedless grape quarters

1 tomato, seeded and chopped

1/3 cup chopped onion

1/3 cup chopped Anaheim chile or
    chopped green chiles

1/4 cup sliced green olives

2 tablespoons chopped fresh cilantro

2 tablespoons olive oil

1 small garlic clove, minced

Salt and pepper to taste

SALMON

1 cup dry white wine

1 cup water

1/2 cup sliced onion

6 peppercorns

1 1/2- to 2-pounds salmon steaks or fillets

To prepare the salsa, combine the grapes, tomato, onion, Anaheim chile, olives, cilantro, olive oil, garlic, salt and pepper in a bowl and mix well. Let stand for 1 hour or longer to allow the flavors to blend.

To prepare the salmon, bring the wine, water, onion and peppercorns to a boil in a skillet. Reduce the heat to low and add the salmon. Poach for 10 minutes per inch of thickness or until the salmon flakes easily when tested with a fork. Remove the salmon from the poaching liquid and let stand until cool. Serve with the salsa.

SERVES 4 TO 6

HONEY MUSTARD SALMON

3 tablespoons Dijon mustard

2 tablespoons honey

4 salmon fillets

1/4 cup chopped fresh tarragon

4 slices tomato

5 teaspoons drained small capers

1/4 cup dry white wine

1/4 cup water

Combine the Dijon mustard and honey in a small bowl and mix well. Arrange the fillets in a single layer in a baking dish and spread the mustard mixture over the top. Sprinkle with 3 tablespoons of the tarragon.

Layer each fillet with one tomato slice and sprinkle with the remaining 1 tablespoon tarragon. Top with the capers. Pour a mixture of the wine and water around the fillets and bake at 400 degrees for 15 minutes or until the fillets flake easily when tested with a fork. Serve immediately.

SERVES 4

ASIAN TILAPIA

4   tilapia fillets
Juice of 2 lemons
1   small piece fresh ginger, peeled and sliced
1/2 cup (about) soy sauce
1/2 cup olive oil

Arrange the fillets in a single layer in a shallow baking dish and drizzle with the lemon juice. Top with the sliced ginger. Bake, covered with foil, at 350 degrees for 20 to 25 minutes or until the fillets flake easily. Remove from the oven and pour the soy sauce over the fillets. Heat the olive oil in a small saucepan over high heat until hot and pour over the fillets. Garnish with green onions and serve immediately.
SERVES 4

SOLE DELICATO

1   (4-ounce) sole fillet
2   to 3 teaspoons olive oil
3   tablespoons (or more) water
3   garlic cloves, thinly sliced
Juice of 1 lemon
Salt and pepper to taste
2   to 3 tablespoons olive oil
5   garlic cloves, sliced
Fresh basil to taste
1   (16-ounce) can peeled tomatoes, drained

Coat both sides of the fillet with 2 to 3 teaspoons of olive oil and arrange in a foil-lined baking pan. Add the water to the baking pan. Sprinkle 3 thinly sliced garlic cloves around the fillet and drizzle the lemon juice on and around the fillet. Sprinkle both sides with salt and pepper and bake at 350 degrees for 15 minutes or until the fillet flakes easily when tested with a fork.

Heat 2 to 3 tablespoons olive oil in a saucepan until hot. Sauté 5 sliced garlic cloves and basil in the hot oil. Add the tomatoes (may add a small amount of juice if desired) and simmer until the tomatoes are cooked down and very tender, stirring occasionally. Arrange the fillet on a serving platter and ladle several spoonfuls of the tomato mixture over the fillet. Garnish with lemon slices, cucumber slices and/or additional fresh basil. Serve with risotto or steamed vegetables and white wine. Quick-and-easy healthful dish.
SERVES 2

PAELLA

1/4	cup olive oil	3	cups Spanish rice
2	tomatoes, chopped	2	envelopes sazón
1	large onion, minced	1	tablespoon chopped fresh parsley
1	bunch scallions, chopped	1	teaspoon salt
2	garlic cloves, minced	1	teaspoon pepper
16	unpeeled large prawns	6	cups chicken broth
16	fresh mussels	4	ounces roasted red bell peppers, julienned
16	small fresh clams		
1 1/2	pounds chopped calamari	1/2	cup white wine
8	ounces baby scallops	1/2	cup cooked green peas
4	ounces chorizo, sliced		

Heat the olive oil in a metal paella pan or large saucepan over medium heat until hot. Sauté the tomatoes, onion, scallions and garlic in the hot oil until the onion is tender. Stir in the prawns and cook until pink. Remove the prawns to a bowl using a slotted spoon, reserving the tomato mixture.

Add the mussels, clams, calamari, scallops and sausage to the reserved tomato mixture and cook over medium heat for 2 minutes. Discard any mussels or clams that do not open. Stir in the rice, sazón, parsley, salt and pepper. Return the prawns along with the broth and roasted bell peppers to the paella pan.

Simmer for 20 minutes or until the liquid is reduced, stirring occasionally. Spoon the paella onto a serving platter and drizzle with the wine. Sprinkle with the peas and let stand for 5 minutes or until the liquid is absorbed.

SERVES 8

SAZÓN is located in the spice section of most grocery stores.
It usually comes in a package that contains three or four envelopes. It is a Hispanic
spice combination that adds ethnic flavors to Spanish-style dishes.

WORTH TASTING

SAUTÉED FLORIDA LOBSTER AND SHRIMP IN KEY LIME SAUCE

KEY LIME SAUCE

2	cups (4 sticks) margarine
4	garlic cloves, minced
1/3	cup Key lime juice
3	to 4 tablespoons hot red pepper sauce

LOBSTER AND SHRIMP

1/4	cup (1/2 stick) margarine
30	large tiger shrimp, peeled and deveined
2	large Florida lobster tails, meat removed and cut into 2-inch pieces
1	pound portobello mushrooms, trimmed and sliced
1/3	cup minced Vidalia onion
1/3	cup chardonnay
5	cups hot cooked wild rice

To prepare the sauce, melt the margarine in a small saucepan over medium heat. Add the garlic and cook for 1 to 2 minutes. Stir in the lime juice and hot sauce. Cook until heated through. Reduce the heat to low and cover to keep warm.

To prepare the lobster and shrimp, melt the margarine in a large saucepan over medium heat. Stir in the shrimp and lobster meat and sauté for 2 to 3 minutes. Add the mushrooms and onion and sauté for 2 minutes. Stir in the wine and Key lime sauce. Cook until the shrimp and lobster are totally coated with the sauce and heated through, stirring frequently. Spoon the lobster mixture over the wild rice on a large serving platter and serve immediately. It is recommended to prep all ingredients first and then prepare the dish.

SERVES 4

WORTH TASTING

BLUE CHEESE AND LOBSTER PASTA

1/2   cup chopped onion

1/2   cup sliced mushrooms

1/4   cup chopped green bell pepper

1/4   cup chopped red bell pepper

6   ounces blue cheese, crumbled

1 1/4   cups half-and-half

4   large Florida lobster tails, meat removed and cut into 2-inch pieces

1/4   cup chopped fresh parsley

1/4   teaspoon pepper

16   ounces thin spaghetti, cooked and drained

Sauté the onion, mushrooms and bell peppers in a large nonstick skillet over medium-low heat until the onion is tender. Stir in the cheese and cook just until the cheese begins to melt. Add the half-and-half and bring to a low boil.

Add the lobster meat to the cheese mixture and cook until the lobster is opaque, stirring occasionally. Stir in the parsley and pepper and spoon over the pasta on a serving platter. Serve immediately. You may substitute shrimp or scallops for the lobster.

SERVES 4

In 1913 SEA GULL COTTAGE *was relocated from its original lakefront community to become part of The Breakers' rental cottages. Sea Gull housed entire families and their staffs for the winter months. It was returned to its lakefront roots in 1983 when The Breakers intended to demolish the building in order to construct condominiums. Once repositioned, approximately two blocks south of its original dwelling, Sea Gull Cottage required a new foundation, a new roof, and extensive woodwork repair. During its seventy-year stay at The Breakers, Sea Gull Cottage was painted white once a year. As a result, what appeared to be intact decorative molding was really several layers of paint over shapeless rotted wood.*

WORTH TASTING

PRAWNS AND PENNE WITH ASPARAGUS

16	ounces penne		1	cup heavy whipping cream
2	tablespoons butter		1	cup (4 ounces) finely grated
2	tablespoons olive oil			Parmesan and Romano cheese
5	shallots, finely chopped		8	ounces fresh asparagus, trimmed and
1/4	cup (about) oil-pack sun-dried			cut into bite-size pieces
	tomatoes, julienned		1/4	cup chopped fresh parsley
3	or 4 garlic cloves, finely chopped		11/2	pounds large prawns or shrimp,
1/2	(750-milliliter) bottle chardonnay			peeled and deveined

Salt and freshly ground pepper to taste

Cook the pasta using the package directions for 8 minutes or until al dente. Drain and cover to keep warm. Heat the butter and olive oil in a large sauté pan over medium-high heat until the butter melts. Stir in the shallots, sun-dried tomatoes and garlic and sauté for 5 minutes or until the shallots and garlic just begin to turn translucent. Stir in the wine and season generously with salt and pepper.

Cook for 5 minutes or until the alcohol evaporates and the mixture is reduced. Stir in the cream and cheese and cook just until the cheese melts, adding additional wine if needed for more sauce. Add the asparagus and cook for 1 minute. Stir in the parsley and shrimp and cook for 3 to 4 minutes or until the shrimp turn pink.

Place the warm pasta on a large platter or in a large pasta bowl. Season with salt and pepper. Spoon the shrimp sauce over the pasta and sprinkle with additional grated Parmesan and Romano cheese and additional chopped fresh parsley. Serve immediately.

Purchase a white wine that you would actually drink when preparing this dish. The better the wine is, the better the dish will be. The same wine you use to prepare the dish is the perfect beverage complement. For variety, substitute lobster or even chicken for the shrimp. If using chicken, chop it into bite-size pieces and add just before the addition of the wine. Reheat leftover pasta in a glass baking dish in the oven at 400 degrees for about 25 to 30 minutes; do not microwave.

SERVES 4 TO 6

BEACHCOMBER SCAMPI

2   tablespoons butter
2   tablespoons all-purpose flour
1   cup canned beef bouillon
2   tablespoons sherry
1/4 cup (1/2 stick) butter
1/4 cup minced shallots
1   cup dry white wine
1/2 cup (1 stick) butter, melted

2   to 3 tablespoons lemon juice
2   tablespoons chopped fresh parsley
2   garlic cloves, crushed
Salt and pepper to taste
36   unpeeled deveined jumbo
        shrimp with tails
Paprika to taste

Melt 2 tablespoons butter in a small saucepan and stir in the flour until blended. Cook over medium heat for 1 to 2 minutes, stirring constantly. Add the bouillon and whisk until combined. Bring to a boil over medium heat, stirring constantly. Remove from the heat and stir in the sherry.

Melt 1/4 cup butter in a 1 1/2-quart saucepan over medium heat. Add the shallots and sauté for about 1 minute. Mix in the wine and cook over medium heat until the mixture is reduced by two-thirds. Stir in the broth mixture and bring to a boil. Remove from the heat and mix in 1/2 cup butter, the lemon juice, parsley, garlic, salt and pepper.

Hold each shrimp so the underside is up. Slice down its length almost to but not through the vein to form the hinge. Spread and flatten to form a butterfly shape and arrange flesh side up in a large shallow baking dish. Sprinkle lightly with salt, pepper and paprika. Spoon the sauce evenly over the shrimp and broil 6 to 8 inches from the heat source for 7 to 8 minutes or until the shrimp turn pink, basting once.

SERVE 6 TO 8

An old favorite from Palm Beach Entertains.

WORTH TASTING

SHRIMP PARMA

1/2	cup olive oil	1	teaspoon dry mustard
2	garlic cloves, finely chopped	1	teaspoon oregano
4	ounces prosciutto, finely chopped	1	teaspoon pepper
1	cup tomato purée		Chopped fresh parsley to taste
1/2	cup red wine	2	pounds peeled shrimp with tails
1	teaspoon salt		Hot cooked rice or pasta

Heat the olive oil in a skillet and add the garlic. Sauté until the garlic is tender but not brown. Stir in the prosciutto and sauté for 1 to 2 minutes. Add the tomato purée, wine, salt, dry mustard, oregano, pepper and parsley and mix well. Cook just until heated through.

Arrange the shrimp in a shallow dish and pour the prosciutto mixture over the shrimp. Marinate in the refrigerator for several hours, turning occasionally. Just before serving, spread the undrained shrimp on a baking sheet with sides and broil for 7 to 9 minutes or until the shrimp turn pink. Serve over rice encircled with French-cut green beans to form a wreath.

SERVES 4

FETA SHRIMP

1	tablespoon plus 1 teaspoon olive oil	1/4	teaspoon chopped fresh rosemary
1	pound shrimp, peeled and deveined	1/2	cup dry white wine
3	garlic cloves, chopped	3	cups sliced grape tomatoes
1	teaspoon dried oregano	3	ounces feta cheese, crumbled
1/2	teaspoon kosher salt	4	cups hot cooked fettuccini
1/4	teaspoon crushed red pepper	1/4	cup chopped fresh parsley

Heat the olive oil in a large skillet over medium-high heat and add the shrimp, garlic, oregano, salt, red pepper and rosemary. Sauté for 2 minutes or until the shrimp are almost cooked through. Spoon the shrimp mixture into a 9×9-inch baking dish coated with additional olive oil.

Deglaze the skillet with the wine. Cook over low heat until reduced by half. Stir in the tomatoes and pour the wine sauce over the shrimp mixture. Sprinkle with the cheese and bake at 350 degrees for 8 to 10 minutes. Spoon the shrimp mixture over the pasta on a serving platter and sprinkle with the parsley.

SERVES 4

WORTH TASTING

RAINY DAY CHEESY SHRIMP

1¹/2	pounds large fresh shrimp	1	tablespoon lemon juice
1¹/2	cups dry white wine	¹/4	teaspoon lemon pepper
¹/4	cup chopped onion	8	ounces lump crab meat, drained and flaked
¹/4	cup finely chopped celery		
1	tablespoon butter	8	ounces fresh mushrooms, sliced
1	teaspoon salt	1	cup soft whole wheat bread crumbs
3	tablespoons butter	¹/4	cup (1 ounce) grated Parmesan cheese
3	tablespoons all-purpose flour		
1	cup half-and-half	¹/4	cup sliced almonds
¹/2	cup (2 ounces) shredded Swiss cheese	2	tablespoons butter, melted
			Hot cooked rice

Peel and devein the shrimp if desired. Combine the wine, onion, celery, 1 tablespoon butter and the salt in a Dutch oven and bring to a boil. Add the shrimp and cook for 3 to 5 minutes or until the shrimp turn pink. Drain, reserving ²/3 cup of the cooking liquid.

Melt 3 tablespoons butter in the Dutch oven over low heat and stir in the flour until smooth. Cook for 1 minute, stirring constantly. Add the half-and-half gradually, whisking constantly. Cook over medium heat until thickened and bubbly, stirring constantly. Add the Swiss cheese and stir until blended. Gradually add the reserved ²/3 cup cooking liquid, lemon juice and lemon pepper and mix well. Stir in the shrimp mixture, crab meat and mushrooms.

Spoon the shrimp mixture into a lightly greased 7×11-inch baking dish. You may prepare in advance to this point and chill, covered, for 8 to 10 hours. Let stand at room temperature for 30 minutes before baking.

Bake, covered, at 350 degrees for 40 minutes. Mix the bread crumbs, Parmesan cheese, almonds and 2 tablespoons butter in a bowl until coated. Sprinkle the crumb mixture over the baked layer and bake for 10 minutes longer. Let stand for 10 minutes before serving. Serve over rice with sliced baguette and a mixed green salad drizzled with a citrus vinaigrette.

SERVES 8

SUNSET SCALLOPS

1   pound scallops
1/2 cup (1 stick) butter, softened
1   tablespoon chopped fresh chives
1   tablespoon chopped fresh parsley
1 1/2 teaspoons celery salt
1   garlic clove, minced
1/2 cup heavy cream
2   egg yolks
1/4 teaspoon curry powder

Rinse the scallops and pat dry. If using sea scallops, which are larger than bay scallops, cut into halves. Combine the butter, chives, parsley, celery salt and garlic in a bowl and mix well. Spread the butter mixture over the bottom of a 7×11-inch baking dish. Arrange the scallops over the prepared layer. Bake at 450 degrees for 10 minutes or until the scallops are opaque.

Beat the cream, egg yolks and curry powder in a mixing bowl until blended and thickened. Spread over the prepared layers and bake for 3 to 5 minutes longer or until light brown. Serve immediately.

SERVES 4

The proposed project of the Ronald McDonald house began in 1989.
The name was later changed to the QUANTUM HOUSE. *Groundbreaking was*
held on September 29, 1998, at St. Mary's Hospital in West Palm Beach.
The Junior League of the Palm Beaches was responsible for the recruiting and training
of volunteers to staff the house. Since Quantum House's opening in the
summer of 2001, the League has helped families by volunteering, supplying food items,
providing janitorial services, redecorating, or just providing comfort.
In 2005 the Quantum House project was set to sunset.

WORTH TASTING

SIDES & SAUCES

Society of the Four Arts

The Society of the Four Arts is a nonprofit organization that was founded in 1936 by a group of Palm Beach residents who felt there was a need for a cultural institution in the community. Its objective is to encourage an appreciation of art, music, drama, and literature.

The original building of the Four Arts was designed by architect Maurice Fatio in 1936. It now houses the Four Arts Library. There is also a gallery named after Esther B. O'Keefe (she is a patron donor to the Society of the Four Arts). This building was designed by architect Addison Mizner. The gallery has been modernized and now contains a 750-seat auditorium to accommodate art exhibitions, concerts, lectures, and films.

The Four Arts Gardens were built in 1938 as a demonstration to show the residents of tropical South Florida the diversity of landscaping. These gardens are maintained by the members of the Palm Beach Garden Club. There are seven themed gardens: the Tropical Fruit Garden, the Chinese Garden, the Spanish Patio, the British Colonial Garden, the Florida Jungle Garden, and the Formal Rose Garden. Each garden contains an appropriate statuary that indicates the architectural style with which it is to be viewed.

The Society of the Four Arts, along with their gardens, also contain the Philip Hulitar Sculpture Garden. Very soon this garden will undergo a dramatic change, as it is being enhanced with new walkways, lighting, and park-like elements. A plaza, fountain, and garden pavilion are planned as focal points for the Sculpture Garden.

Gallery Night
A Palette of Taste

SUNSET SANGRIA

PALM BEACH PESTO SAUCE WITH BRIE

MELON BALLS WITH CREAMY YOGURT FRUIT DIP

MIDSUMMER NIGHT'S SALAD

PERFECT PRIME RIB

ROASTED SWEET POTATO FRIES WITH SAVORY DILL DIP

SPRING RISOTTO WITH PEAS AND ZUCCHINI

RUM CAKE

Chianti, Classico, Tuscany*

* see page 171

TARRAGON-ROASTED ASPARAGUS TIPS

2   pounds fresh asparagus spears
1/4   cup fresh lemon juice
3   tablespoons extra-virgin olive oil
2   tablespoons water

1   shallot, finely chopped
1   teaspoon chopped fresh tarragon
Salt and pepper to taste

Snap off the thick woody ends of the asparagus spears; the spears should be approximately 4 to 5 inches long. Arrange the asparagus in a single layer on a baking sheet.

Mix the lemon juice, olive oil, water, shallot and tarragon in a bowl and pour over the asparagus, turning to coat. Sprinkle with salt and pepper and roast at 375 degrees for 15 to 17 minutes or until light brown.

SERVES 8

GARLICKY GREEN BEANS

1 1/2 to 2 pounds fresh green beans
1   onion, chopped
2   or 3 slices bacon
3   or 4 garlic cloves

2   tablespoons butter
1/8   teaspoon garlic powder
Salt and pepper to taste

Break off the ends of the green beans. Combine the beans, onion, bacon and garlic cloves with enough water to cover in a large saucepan. Bring to a boil and reduce the heat to low.

Simmer, partially covered, for 25 to 30 minutes or until the beans are tender; drain. Discard the bacon and garlic cloves and stir in the butter. Season with the garlic powder, salt and pepper.

SERVES 4 TO 6

WORTH TASTING

ROQUEFORT SOUFFLÉ

Butter for coating
Grated Parmesan cheese for sprinkling

1	cup milk
3	tablespoons unsalted butter
3	tablespoons all-purpose flour
1/2	teaspoon kosher salt
1/4	teaspoon freshly ground black pepper
1/8	teaspoon cayenne pepper
1/8	teaspoon ground nutmeg
4	egg yolks, at room temperature and beaten
5	ounces Roquefort cheese, crumbled
1/4	cup (1 ounce) grated Parmesan cheese
5	egg whites, at room temperature
1/8	teaspoon cream of tartar
1/8	teaspoon salt

Preheat the oven to 400 degrees. Coat an 8-cup soufflé dish with butter and sprinkle with grated Parmesan cheese. Scald or heat the milk in a saucepan until just below the boiling point; do not boil. Melt 3 tablespoons butter in a small saucepan over low heat. Stir in the flour using a wooden spoon and cook for 2 minutes, stirring constantly. Remove from the heat and whisk in the scalded milk, 1/2 teaspoon salt, the black pepper, cayenne pepper and nutmeg.

Cook over low heat for 1 minute or until thickened, whisking constantly. Remove from the heat. Whisk a small amount of the hot mixture into the egg yolks and then whisk the egg yolks into the hot mixture. Mix in the Roquefort cheese and 1/4 cup Parmesan cheese and pour into a large mixing bowl.

Beat the egg whites, cream of tartar and 1/8 teaspoon salt in a mixing bowl at low speed for 1 minute. Increase the speed to medium and beat for 1 minute. Increase the speed to high and beat until stiff glossy peaks form. Fold the egg whites into the cheese mixture one-fourth at a time, mixing after each addition just until combined.

Pour the soufflé mixture into the prepared soufflé dish. Reduce the oven temperature to 375 degrees and bake for 30 to 35 minutes or until puffed and brown; do not peek. Serve immediately. Serve as a side dish with beef fillet or your favorite cut of beef.

SERVES 6

SAUTÉED BRUSSELS SPROUTS

6   ounces turkey bacon
2¹/2 tablespoons olive oil
1¹/2 pounds brussels sprouts, trimmed and
        cut into halves
³/4 teaspoon kosher salt

³/4 teaspoon freshly ground pepper
1³/4 cups (or more) chicken broth
³/4 cup golden raisins
Salt and pepper to taste

Heat a 12-inch sauté pan over medium-low heat and add the bacon. Cook over medium heat for 3 to 4 minutes per side or until the bacon is brown and crisp. Remove the bacon to a paper towel to drain, reserving the bacon drippings in the pan. Break the bacon into ¹/4-inch pieces.

Heat the olive oil with the reserved bacon drippings and add the brussels sprouts, ³/4 teaspoon salt and ³/4 teaspoon pepper. Sauté over medium heat for 5 minutes or until light brown. Stir in the broth and raisins. Decrease the heat and cook for 15 minutes (20 to 25 minutes for large brussels sprouts) or until the brussels sprouts are tender when pierced with a knife, adding additional chicken broth or water if the skillet becomes too dry. Return the bacon to the skillet and cook until heated through. Season with salt and pepper and serve immediately.

SERVES 6

CREAMY CORN PUDDING

1   (8-ounce) package corn muffin mix
1   (8-ounce) can cream-style corn
1   (8-ounce) can white kernel
        corn, drained
1   cup sour cream

¹/2 cup (1 stick) butter or margarine,
        melted
2   eggs, lightly beaten
1   cup (4 ounces) shredded Swiss cheese

Combine the muffin mix, cream-style corn, white corn, sour cream, butter and eggs in a bowl and mix well. Spoon the corn mixture into an 8×8-inch baking pan and bake at 350 degrees for 40 minutes. Sprinkle with the cheese and bake for 10 minutes longer. Serve hot.

SERVE 8 TO 10

WORTH TASTING

COLORFUL COUSCOUS

1   cup slivered almonds
2   cups instant couscous
2   cups boiling water
1   tablespoon olive oil
1   cup dried apricots, thinly sliced
1/2 cup golden raisins
1/2 cup dried cranberries
1/4 cup coarsely chopped fresh mint
1   tablespoon ground cumin
6   tablespoons olive oil
6   tablespoons lemon juice
Salt and pepper to taste

Spread the almonds on a baking sheet and toast at 400 degrees until light brown. Remove the almonds to a plate to cool. Combine the couscous and boiling water in a heatproof bowl and mix well. Let stand for 15 minutes and then fluff with a fork. Coat your hands with 1 tablespoon olive oil and gently break up any lumps.

Stir the apricots, raisins, cranberries, mint and cumin into the couscous. Add 6 tablespoons olive oil and the lemon juice and mix well. Season with salt and pepper. Serve warm or chilled. Great with lamb.

SERVES 6 TO 8

COUSCOUS *is a grain dish made with crushed wheat or rice. It is a staple in the Middle East and North Africa and is the national dish of Morocco. Although Arab in modern times, couscous historically is from China.*

WORTH TASTING

TRIPLE-CHEESE EGGPLANT PARMESAN

5	eggs		15	ounces ricotta cheese
1	teaspoon parsley flakes		1	egg, lightly beaten
1/8	teaspoon salt		1	cup (4 ounces) grated
1/8	teaspoon pepper			Parmesan cheese
1/8	teaspoon garlic powder		1	tablespoon chopped
1/8	teaspoon onion powder			fresh parsley
2	large eggplant, peeled and		1/8	teaspoon pepper
	cut into rounds		1/8	teaspoon onion powder

Italian-seasoned bread crumbs
    for coating
Extra-virgin olive oil for frying
1 1/2 pounds mozzarella cheese,
    shredded

1 (26-ounce) can or jar of
    spaghetti sauce
1 teaspoon parsley flakes
Pepper to taste

Whisk 5 eggs, 1 teaspoon parsley flakes, the salt, 1/8 teaspoon pepper, the garlic powder and
1/8 teaspoon onion powder in a bowl until combined. Dip the eggplant slices in the egg mixture until
coated and then coat with bread crumbs.

Pour enough olive oil into a skillet to measure 1/4 inch. Heat over medium-high heat until hot.
Fry the coated eggplant slices in batches in the hot oil until golden brown on both sides, adding additional
olive oil as needed; drain. Mix 1/2 cup of the mozzarella cheese, the ricotta cheese, 1 egg, 1 tablespoon
of the Parmesan cheese, 1 tablespoon fresh parsley, 1/8 teaspoon pepper and 1/8 teaspoon onion powder
in a bowl.

Spread a thin layer of the spaghetti sauce over the bottom of a 10×12-inch baking dish. Arrange half
the eggplant slices in rows over the spaghetti sauce and spread with another thin layer of the spaghetti
sauce. Sprinkle with half the remaining Parmesan cheese and spread with half the ricotta cheese mixture.
Sprinkle with half the remaining mozzarella cheese. Arrange the remaining eggplant slices in rows over
the prepared layers. Layer with a thin layer of spaghetti sauce, the remaining Parmesan cheese, the remaining
ricotta cheese mixture and the remaining mozzarella cheese. Sprinkle with 1 teaspoon parsley flakes and
pepper to taste and bake at 375 degrees until golden brown and bubbly around the edges. Let stand for
10 minutes before serving.

SERVES 10 TO 12

WORTH TASTING

GARLICKY POTATOES WITH LIME

1 pound unpeeled small red potatoes, sliced	1 tablespoon oregano, crushed
	Finely grated zest and juice of 1 lime
1 tablespoon extra-virgin olive oil	1 tablespoon chopped fresh parsley
1 red bell pepper, thinly sliced	Salt and pepper to taste
4 garlic cloves, crushed	Paprika to taste

Steam the potatoes in a steamer for 8 to 10 minutes or until tender; drain. Heat the olive oil in a skillet and add the bell pepper, garlic and oregano. Sauté over medium heat for 2 to 3 minutes or until the bell peppers begin to soften. Add the potatoes and stir to coat. Sprinkle with the lime zest and drizzle with the lime juice. Add the parsley and toss to mix. Season with salt, pepper and paprika.

SERVES 4

HERB-ROASTED POTATOES POUPON

5 tablespoons Dijon mustard	1/2 teaspoon Italian seasoning
2 tablespoons olive oil	2 green onions, chopped
1 garlic clove, chopped	6 red potatoes (2 pounds)

Combine the Dijon mustard, olive oil, garlic, Italian seasoning and green onions in a bowl and mix well. Arrange the potatoes in a lightly greased 9×13-inch baking pan or on a shallow baking sheet.

Drizzle the mustard mixture over the potatoes and toss to coat. Roast at 425 degrees for 35 to 40 minutes or until tender.

SERVES 6 TO 8

*The JUNIOR COTILLION was organized in 1958 by the Junior League
of the Palm Beaches to provide etiquette and dance training to children in
Palm Beach County. The Cotillion Program, a major fund-raiser
for the Junior League, is still in existence today, preparing sixth and
seventh graders to be socially graceful.*

WORTH TASTING

ISLAND COCONUT RICE

1	(14-ounce) can coconut milk
1	cup jasmine rice
1/4	cup water
1/2	teaspoon salt
1/2	teaspoon honey
1/2	teaspoon crushed red pepper flakes
1/8	teaspoon turmeric
1	teaspoon minced fresh ginger

Combine the coconut milk, rice, water, salt, honey, red pepper flakes and turmeric in a large saucepan and mix well. Bring to a boil over medium heat, stirring constantly. Reduce the heat to low.

Simmer, covered, for 20 minutes. Fluff the rice with a fork and spoon into a serving bowl. Sprinkle with the ginger. Garnish with sliced almonds and serve immediately.

SERVES 4

RICE PILAF

1/2	cup (1 stick) butter or margarine
8	ounces fresh mushrooms, sliced
3/4	cup rice
1/2	onion, chopped
3/4	teaspoon paprika
3/4	teaspoon oregano
1	(10-ounce) can beef consommé
3/4	cup water
1/2	cup sherry

Melt the butter in a saucepan and add the mushrooms, rice, onion, paprika and oregano. Simmer for 20 minutes, stirring occasionally. Spoon the rice mixture into a baking dish and stir in the consommé, water and sherry. Bake, covered, at 400 degrees for 45 minutes. Remove the cover and bake for 15 minutes longer.

SERVES 6

SPRING RISOTTO WITH PEAS AND ZUCCHINI

2   (14-ounce) cans reduced-sodium chicken broth

2 1/2 cups water

2   tablespoons butter

1   or 2 large zucchini (1 pound), cut into 1/2-inch pieces

Coarse salt and freshly ground pepper to taste

1/2 cup finely chopped onion

1   teaspoon salt

1/4 teaspoon pepper

1 1/2 cups arborio rice

1/2 cup dry white wine or chicken broth

1   cup frozen peas, thawed

1/2 cup (2 ounces) grated Parmesan cheese

1   tablespoon butter

Heat the broth and water in a small saucepan over low heat. Cover to keep warm. Melt 2 tablespoons butter in a 3-quart saucepan over medium heat and stir in the zucchini. Season with salt and pepper to taste. Cook for 8 to 10 minutes or until the zucchini is golden brown, stirring constantly. Remove the zucchini to a bowl using a slotted spoon, reserving the pan drippings.

Reduce the heat to medium-low and stir the onion into the reserved pan drippings. Cook for 5 minutes or until tender. Stir in 1 teaspoon salt and 1/4 teaspoon pepper. Increase the heat to medium and add the rice. Cook for 3 minutes or until the rice is translucent around the edges. Mix in the wine and cook for 2 minutes or until the wine is absorbed.

Continue cooking and add the heated broth 1 cup at a time, stirring until the broth is almost absorbed after each addition and the rice is tender. The process should take about 25 to 30 minutes. Stir in the zucchini and peas and cook for 2 minutes or until the peas are bright green. Remove from the heat and stir in the cheese and 1 tablespoon butter. Serve topped with additional cheese.

Arborio rice makes the creamiest risotto. If this type of rice is not available in your supermarket, substitute with medium grain or long grain white rice.

SERVES 6

WORTH TASTING

RISOTTO MILANESE

5	cups chicken broth
2	tablespoons olive oil
1	small onion, minced
2	cups arborio rice
1/16	teaspoon saffron
	Salt and pepper to taste
1/4	cup (1 ounce) grated Parmesan cheese
1 1/2	tablespoons butter or margarine

Heat the broth in a saucepan over high heat until hot but not simmering. Reduce the heat to low and cover to keep warm. Heat the olive oil in a Dutch oven over medium heat. Sauté the onion in the hot oil until golden brown and tender. Add the rice and stir until coated.

Increase the heat and stir in 1 cup of the warm broth. Cook until all of the broth is absorbed, stirring constantly. Add 1 cup of the remaining warm broth and cook until all of the broth is absorbed, stirring constantly. Sprinkle in the saffron.

Continue cooking and adding enough of the remaining warm broth 1 cup at a time until the rice is al dente, stirring constantly until the broth is absorbed after each addition. Taste and season with salt and pepper. Remove from the heat and stir in the cheese and butter. Serve as an entrée with mixed salad greens.

SERVES 4

E.R. Bradley opened BRADLEY'S BEACH CLUB *in 1898, at which time it was considered the most exclusive casino in the world. The membership was restricted to extremely wealthy non-Florida residents and was one of the first private casinos to allow women to gamble. Members were allowed to dine at the extravagant restaurant. Prices were not listed on the menu, and any dish could be created upon request. Upon his death in 1946, Bradley donated the club's land to the Town of Palm Beach as a public park.*

WORTH TASTING

ROASTED SWEET POTATO FRIES WITH SAVORY DILL DIP

SAVORY DILL DIP

1 cup sour cream

1/2 cup mayonnaise

2 tablespoons chopped fresh dill weed, or to taste

1 tablespoon lemon juice

1 teaspoon garlic salt

SWEET POTATO FRIES

4 to 6 sweet potatoes, cut into strips

Olive oil to taste

Seasoned salt to taste

Salt and pepper to taste

To prepare the dip, combine the sour cream, mayonnaise, dill weed, lemon juice and garlic salt in a bowl and mix well.

To prepare the fries, spread the sweet potatoes in a single layer on a 10×15-inch baking sheet and drizzle with olive oil. Sprinkle with seasoned salt, salt and pepper and roast at 400 degrees for 30 minutes or until slightly crisp, turning halfway through the roasting process. Serve immediately with the dip.

SERVES 4 TO 6

THE CONGRESSMAN'S SWEET POTATOES

3 or 4 (about) sweet potatoes

1/2 cup granulated sugar

1/2 cup milk

1/4 cup (1/2 stick) butter, softened

2 eggs, lightly beaten

1 teaspoon vanilla extract

3/4 cup packed brown sugar

1/3 cup all-purpose flour

5 tablespoons butter, melted

11/4 cups chopped pecans

Place the sweet potatoes on a baking sheet and bake at 450 degrees for 1 hour. Reduce the oven temperature to 275 degrees. Cool the sweet potatoes until easily handled. Scoop the pulp into a bowl and mash; the pulp should measure 31/2 cups. Stir in the granulated sugar, milk, 1/4 cup butter, the eggs and vanilla until combined. Spoon the sweet potato mixture into a 2-quart baking dish.

Mix the brown sugar, flour, 5 tablespoons butter and the pecans in a bowl and spread over the prepared layer. Bake, covered, for 20 minutes. Remove the cover and bake for 10 minutes longer.

SERVES 10

TOMATO BASIL TART

1	unbaked (9-inch) pie shell		1	cup (4 ounces) shredded mozzarella cheese
1	cup fresh basil		1/2	cup mayonnaise
4	garlic cloves		1/4	cup (1 ounce) grated Parmesan cheese
1/2	cup (2 ounces) shredded mozzarella cheese		1/8	teaspoon pepper
5	or 6 plum tomatoes, seeded and cut into 1/4-inch slices			

Line the pie shell with foil and bake at 450 degrees for 5 minutes. Remove the foil and bake for 8 minutes longer. Reduce the oven temperature to 350 degrees. Process the basil and garlic in a food processor until chopped.

Sprinkle 1/2 cup mozzarella cheese over the bottom of the baked pie shell. Layer the tomatoes over the cheese and sprinkle with the basil mixture. Mix 1 cup mozzarella cheese, the mayonnaise, Parmesan cheese and pepper in a bowl and spread over the tomatoes. Bake for 20 minutes or until golden brown. Cool slightly and cut into wedges.

SERVES 8

SPICY MEXI-CALI SAUCE

1/2	cup mayonnaise		1/4	teaspoon salt
1/2	cup sour cream		1/4	teaspoon dried dill weed
2	tablespoons heavy cream		1/4	teaspoon paprika
1	tablespoon white vinegar		1/4	teaspoon cayenne pepper
2	teaspoons minced jalapeño chile		1/4	teaspoon ground cumin
2	teaspoons minced onion		1/4	teaspoon chili powder
1/2	teaspoon parsley flakes		1/8	teaspoon garlic powder
1/2	teaspoon Tabasco sauce		1/8	teaspoon freshly ground black pepper

Combine the mayonnaise, sour cream, heavy cream, vinegar, jalapeño chile and onion in a bowl and mix well. Stir in the parsley flakes, Tabasco sauce, salt, dill weed, paprika, cayenne pepper, cumin, chili powder, garlic powder and black pepper. Serve with Margarita Chicken on page 102. Or, serve as a dip with chips, crackers and/or chopped fresh vegetables.

SERVES 8

DELICATO SAUCE

3 tablespoons olive oil

Garlic to taste, sliced or chopped

2 handfuls of fresh basil leaves

2 tablespoons butter

2 (16-ounce) cans peeled
  tomatoes, drained

1/16 teaspoon salt

1/2 cup half-and-half or cream

Freshly grated Parmesan cheese
  to taste

Hot cooked penne

Heat the olive oil in a saucepan over low heat. Cook the garlic in the hot oil and then stir in the basil. Cook until the basil begins to wilt and then stir in the butter. Add the tomatoes and mash until combined with the basil mixture.

Simmer for 5 to 10 minutes or until the tomato mixture is cooked down, stirring constantly. Stir in the salt and half-and-half. Add cheese and mix well. Spoon over pasta and garnish with sprigs of basil and freshly grated Parmesan cheese. Serve immediately.

SERVES 4

French haute cuisine consists of stocks and sauces. Sauces are stocks with different ingredients in them. Marie-Antoine Carême, a founder of French haute cuisine, pointed out that most sauces were variations of several basic sauces. These are known as the five MOTHER SAUCES. *All other variations stem from these. They are:*

BÉCHAMEL SAUCE *is a white cream sauce made from butter, flour, and milk. From béchamel comes Mornay sauce.* ESPAGNOLE SAUCE *is also called brown sauce or demi-glace. It is made from beef stock, butter, flour, and herbs. The base is cooked a long time, which gives the sauce the brown color and nutty flavor.* HOLLANDAISE SAUCE *is made with butter, egg yolks, and lemon juice. It is a rich buttery sauce related to bernaise sauce and well-known for its importance in eggs Benedict.* VELOUTÉ SAUCE *is made with butter, flour, and either chicken, veal, or fish stock. It is served with poultry or fish. From velouté sauce comes Allemande Sauce, which has lemon juice, egg yolks, and cream added.* TOMATO SAUCE *is a red sauce made of tomatoes, onions, basil, salt, oil, garlic, and spices. The sauce is coarse because the tomatoes are broiled, peeled, strained, and puréed.*

WORTH TASTING

MARCHAND DU VIN SAUCE

3/4 cup (1 1/2 sticks) butter
1/2 cup finely chopped onion
1/3 cup finely chopped shallots
    or scallions
1 tablespoon minced garlic
2 tablespoons chopped fresh parsley
1 pound mushrooms, sliced

3/4 cup beef stock
1/2 cup burgundy or chianti
1 tablespoon Kitchen Bouquet
1/2 teaspoon salt
1/8 teaspoon black pepper
1/8 teaspoon cayenne pepper
2 tablespoons cornstarch (optional)

Combine the butter, onion, shallots, garlic and parsley in a saucepan. Simmer until the onion is tender but not brown. Add the mushrooms, stock, wine, Kitchen Bouquet, salt, black pepper and cayenne pepper and mix well.

Simmer for 30 minutes, stirring occasionally. Stir in a mixture of the cornstarch and a small amount of water and cook until thickened, stirring frequently. Taste and adjust the seasonings. Simmer for 30 minutes longer. Serve over beef tenderloin. You may freeze for future use.

MAKES 2 CUPS

PALM BEACH PESTO SAUCE

2 cups fresh basil leaves
1/2 cup extra-virgin olive oil
2 tablespoons pine nuts

1 or 2 garlic cloves
1/2 cup (2 ounces) grated Romano cheese
2 tablespoons butter

Combine the basil, olive oil, pine nuts, garlic and cheese in a food processor. Pulse until of the desired consistency. Add the butter and process until combined. Serve over hot cooked pasta, on crackers with Brie cheese or other cheeses or over potatoes. Add to soups for extra flavor.

SERVES 6

WORTH TASTING

DESSERTS

Ann Norton House and Sculpture Gardens

The Ann Norton Sculpture Gardens, the former home of the late Ann Weaver Norton, has become a "must-see" collection for art lovers worldwide. Norton was a student at the National Academy of Design and Cooper Union Art School in New York City in her youth. She later moved to West Palm Beach, Florida, where she utilized stone, wood, and bronze as her media to create the magnificent gardens that have become a landmark site in South Florida.

This sanctuary, founded in 1977 by the artist, is composed of three magnificent gardens. Each of the gardens was created to display Ann Norton's colossal sculptures with a background of unusual tropical plants and a collection of more than three hundred varieties of palm trees. By creating this environment, Ann Norton ensured that all visitors to her home would find something to pique their interest.

Today her home and garden area house more than one hundred sculptures created solely by the artist. Throughout her life, Norton's passion for sculpture and love for the arts were the forces behind defining the breathtaking landscape surrounding her home, which is currently listed in the National Register of Historic Places. In addition, she was the driving force behind the present-day annual program of exhibitions by internationally known artists. Ann Norton's dedication to the art world has provided an environment to be enjoyed by all.

Garden Tea Party

PALM BEACH PUNCH

CHEDDAR DATES

TEQUESTA TEA SANDWICHES

TOMATO BASIL TART

PUMPKIN SCONES WITH CRANBERRY BUTTER

MINIATURE CREAM CHEESE DELIGHTS

APPLE PIE CRISP

BROWNIE TRIFLE

FRESH FRUIT PIZZA

Pinot Gris, Alsace, France*

* see page 171

ALMOND CHEESECAKE

GRAHAM CRACKER CRUST

1¹/2 cups graham cracker crumbs

2 tablespoons sugar

1 teaspoon all-purpose flour

1/4 cup (1/2 stick) butter, melted

CHEESECAKE FILLING

32 ounces cream cheese, softened

1 cup sugar

2 eggs

1/2 teaspoon vanilla extract

1/2 teaspoon almond extract

SOUR CREAM TOPPING

2 cups sour cream

3/4 cup sugar

3/4 teaspoon almond extract

1/2 teaspoon lemon juice

To prepare the crust, combine the graham cracker crumbs, sugar, flour and butter in a bowl and mix well. Pat the crumb mixture in a 10-inch springform pan. Bake at 350 degrees for 5 minutes. Remove to a wire rack to cool. Turn off the oven and open the door to allow the oven to cool.

To prepare the filling, combine the cream cheese, sugar, eggs, and flavorings in a mixing bowl and beat until blended. Spread the cream cheese filling over the baked crust. Place the springform pan in a cold oven and turn the oven to 350 degrees. Bake for 30 minutes. Maintain the oven temperature.

To prepare the topping, combine the sour cream, sugar, flavoring and lemon juice in a bowl and mix well. Spread the sour cream mixture over the baked layers and bake for 8 minutes longer. Chill, covered, for 8 to 10 hours before serving.

SERVES 18 TO 20

An old favorite from Palm Beach Entertains.

WORTH TASTING

MARGARITA CHEESECAKE

PRETZEL CRUST

1¹/2 cups crushed pretzels
2   tablespoons sugar
¹/4   cup (¹/2 stick) butter, melted

CHEESECAKE

1¹/2 envelopes unflavored gelatin
³/4   cup sugar
³/4   cup water

24   ounces cream cheese, softened
³/4   cup sour cream
¹/4   cup fresh lime juice
¹/4   cup tequila
¹/4   cup Grand Mariner or Triple Sec
1¹/2 teaspoons finely grated lime zest
¹/4   teaspoon salt

To prepare the crust, process the pretzels in a food processor until finely ground; the crumbs should measure about 1 cup. Add the sugar and pulse until combined. Add the butter and process just until mixed. Press the crumb mixture over the bottom and up the side of a 9-inch springform pan. Bake at 375 degrees for 5 minutes or until set. Remove to a wire rack to cool.

To prepare the cheesecake, soften the gelatin in a small amount of cold water in a bowl. Combine the gelatin mixture and sugar in a small saucepan. Stir in ³/4 cup water and cook over medium heat for 3 minutes or until the gelatin and sugar dissolve. Let stand until cool.

Beat the cream cheese in a mixing bowl until smooth, scraping the bowl occasionally. Add the sour cream, lime juice, tequila, liqueur, lime zest and salt and beat until combined. Mix in the gelatin mixture. Spread the cream cheese mixture over the baked crust and chill for 4 to 5 hours or until set. Remove the side of the pan. Dip the bottom of thinly cut lime slices in additional sugar and arrange around the outer edge of the cheesecake if desired. Garnish with strips of lime zest.

SERVES 10

---

*Who is Margarita? She was a lovely young bride who received a
cocktail named after her as a wedding gift. The basic* MARGARITA *is one-third
tequila, one-third Triple Sec, and one-third fresh lime juice.*

WORTH TASTING

MINIATURE CREAM CHEESE DELIGHTS

1	package graham cracker pie crust mix
16	ounces cream cheese, softened
1/2	cup sugar
2	eggs
1	teaspoon vanilla extract
1	(21-ounce) can cherry pie filling

Prepare the pie crust mix using the package directions. Press 1 teaspoon or more of the crust mixture over the bottom of each of forty-eight paper-lined miniature muffin cups. Process the cream cheese, sugar, eggs and vanilla in a blender for 30 seconds.

Fill the prepared muffin cups two-thirds full with the cream cheese mixture. Bake at 350 degrees for 20 to 30 minutes or until set. Top with the pie filling. Chill until serving time.

MAKES 4 DOZEN

APPLE PIE CRISP

1	(2-layer) package yellow cake mix
1/2	cup (1 stick) butter, melted
1	egg, lightly beaten
2	(21-ounce) cans apple pie filling
8	ounces cream cheese, softened
3	eggs, lightly beaten
1	(2-layer) package butter-recipe cake mix
1/2	cup (1 stick) butter, melted

Combine the yellow cake mix, 1/2 cup butter and 1 egg in a bowl and mix well. Press over the bottom of a 9×13-inch baking pan.

Combine the pie filling, cream cheese and 3 eggs in a bowl and mix well. Spread the pie filling mixture over the prepared layer. Sprinkle with the butter-recipe cake mix and drizzle with 1/2 cup butter. Bake at 350 degrees for 1 hour or until golden brown.

SERVES 10

DESSERTS

WORTH TASTING

APPLE PEAR DELIGHT

1/4	cup bourbon or apple cider	1/2	cup sugar
2	tablespoons lemon juice	3/4	teaspoon ground cinnamon
1	tablespoon water	1/2	teaspoon ground allspice
1	teaspoon vanilla extract	1/8	teaspoon salt
3	Granny Smith apples, peeled and sliced	1/4	cup chopped nuts
		2	tablespoons fat-free unsalted butter
3	ripe pears, peeled and sliced	2	tablespoons vegetable oil
1	cup all-purpose flour		Whipped topping

Mix the bourbon, lemon juice, water and vanilla in a bowl. Add the apples and pears and toss to coat. Spoon the apple mixture into a 7×12-inch baking dish.

Combine the flour, sugar, cinnamon, allspice, salt and nuts in a bowl and mix well. Cut the butter into the flour mixture using two knives until crumbly. Stir in the oil and spoon over the prepared layer. Bake at 350 degrees for 30 minutes. If there is juice spoon over the top and bake for 15 to 20 minutes longer or until the fruit is tender and the topping is brown and crisp. Spoon into dessert bowls and top with whipped topping.

SERVES 12

CRANBERRY APPLE CRISP

3	cups chopped peeled apples	3/4	cup chopped pecans
2	cups fresh cranberries	1/2	cup all-purpose flour
2	tablespoons all-purpose flour	1/2	cup packed brown sugar
1	cup granulated sugar	1/2	cup (1 stick) butter or margarine, melted
3	envelopes instant oatmeal mix with cinnamon and spice		

Toss the apples and cranberries with 2 tablespoons flour in a bowl. Stir in the granulated sugar and spoon the apple mixture into a 2-quart baking dish.

Mix the oatmeal mix, chopped pecans, 1/2 cup flour and the brown sugar in a bowl. Stir in the butter and spoon the pecan mixture over the prepared layer. Bake at 350 degrees for 45 minutes. Garnish with pecan halves.

SERVES 4

FLAN

¹/2 cup sugar
1 (14-ounce) can sweetened condensed milk
1 (12-ounce) can evaporated milk
5 eggs
1 teaspoon vanilla extract
¹/4 teaspoon salt

Heat the sugar in a saucepan over medium heat until liquefied and caramel in color. Pour into a 2-quart foil pan with a lip, approximately 3¹/2-inches deep. To make a water bath, use a large ovenproof saucepan that will accommodate the foil pan sitting on top; the lipped foil pan works best for this. Add water to the saucepan until the water reaches almost to the top of the foil pan when placed on top of the saucepan.

Process the condensed milk, evaporated milk, eggs, vanilla and salt in a blender until smooth and pour the milk mixture over the caramelized sugar. Bake, covered with foil, at 250 degrees for 3 hours. Remove the foil pan from the saucepan and chill in the refrigerator. Just before serving invert onto a serving platter.

The bain-marie, or water bath technique, is used for custards, cheesecakes and melting chocolate.

SERVES 8

---

*In 1959 The Junior League of the Palm Beaches organized the Junior Museum Guild
to create a science museum in Palm Beach County. The museum was renamed*
THE SOUTH FLORIDA SCIENCE MUSEUM AND PLANETARIUM *in 1963. In 2003
the Junior League created the 4U2 Discover Program, whereby hundreds
of needy children are afforded a free day at the museum. The Science Museum continues
to be an educational interactive museum for children of all ages. In 2006
groundbreaking occurred for the Dekelbaum Science Center, a new state-of-the-art facility.*

WORTH TASTING

BERRYLICIOUS ANGEL FOOD

8   ounces light whipped topping
3/4 (8-ounce) container lemon chiffon light yogurt
1   angel food cake
Sliced fresh strawberries
Fresh blueberries
Fresh raspberries

Combine the whipped topping and yogurt in a serving bowl and mix well. Break the angel food cake into bite-size pieces and fold into the whipped topping mixture. Add the strawberries, blueberries and raspberries and mix gently. Chill, covered, for 30 to 60 minutes and spoon into dessert bowls.
SERVES 4 TO 6

Angel food cake versus devil's food cake. ANGEL FOOD CAKE *is
said to be so light and fluffy that it is fit for an angel to eat.
It is made predominately with beaten egg whites. Beat room temperature
egg whites in a clean dry bowl for maximum volume.*
DEVIL'S FOOD CAKE *is the opposite. It has more chocolate than regular
chocolate cake, and is so rich and delicious that it is almost sinful.*

WORTH TASTING

BROWNIE TRIFLE

1 (21-ounce) package fudge brownie mix
1/4 cup praline liqueur or coffee liqueur
1 (16-ounce) package miniature Heath bars
1 (2-ounce) package fudge instant pudding mix
12 ounces whipped topping

Prepare the brownie mix using the package directions. Pierce the top of the warm brownies at 1-inch intervals and brush with the liqueur. Let stand until cool and then crumble into small pieces.

Process the candy bars in a food processor until crushed or place in a sealable plastic bag and crush using a rolling pin. Prepare the pudding mix, omitting the chilling step. Layer the brownie pieces, pudding, candy bars and whipped topping half at a time in a trifle bowl. Chill, covered, for 8 hours or longer before serving. Garnish with chocolate curls.

SERVES 12

CHOCOLATE ZABAGLIONE

1/2 cup (3 ounces) semisweet chocolate chips
1/4 cup whipping cream or heavy cream
8 egg yolks
3/4 cup sugar
2/3 cup dry marsala
1/8 teaspoon salt
1 pound fresh strawberries, cut into quarters

Combine the chocolate chips and cream in a small heavy saucepan. Cook over medium heat until blended, stirring frequently. Remove from the heat and cover to keep warm.

Whisk the egg yolks, sugar, wine and salt in a large heatproof bowl until blended. Set the bowl over a saucepan of simmering water; do not allow the bottom of the bowl to touch the water. Cook over the simmering water for 4 minutes or until thick and creamy, whisking constantly. Remove from the heat and fold the chocolate mixture into the egg mixture using a large spatula. Divide the strawberries evenly among six coupe dishes. Pour the warm zabaglione over the strawberries and serve immediately.

Zabaglione is an Italian dessert that resembles a very light whipped custard. In France, the same dessert is called sabayon.

SERVES 6

WORTH TASTING

MELBA SAUCE OVER ICE CREAM

1 (10-ounce) package frozen raspberries, thawed

1/2 cup red currant jelly

1/4 cup (or less) sugar

1 tablespoon fresh lemon juice

1/4 teaspoon finely grated lemon zest

1/8 teaspoon salt

12 flat round crisp cookies

Vanilla ice cream

Place the raspberries in a saucepan. Simmer, covered, for 15 minutes. Strain into a large glass measuring cup through a sieve, pressing gently to extract all of the juice. Discard the seeds and pulp. Add enough water to the juice to measure 2/3 cup. Stir in the jelly, half the sugar, the lemon juice, lemon zest and salt. Taste and add the desired amount of the remaining sugar if desired. Let stand until cool and then chill, covered, in the refrigerator.

Arrange the cookies in a single layer on a baking sheet lined with foil. Top each cookie with a large scoop of ice cream and freeze until firm. To serve, arrange the ice cream–topped cookies on individual dessert plates and spoon 2 tablespoon of the sauce over each. This is a very simple but decadent dessert that will surprise your guests.

SERVES 12

MELBA SAUCE *was named after a famous Australian soprano*
whose stage name came from her hometown of Melbourne, Australia. She shortened
her name to Melba. A famous chef in London created the dessert
Peach Melba in her honor. Melba toast was also named after her when a waiter
served her a thin piece of burnt toast, which she loved.

WORTH TASTING

FRESH FRUIT PIZZA

1	(14-ounce) can sweetened condensed milk
1/2	cup sour cream
1/4	cup lemon juice
1	teaspoon vanilla extract
1/2	cup (1 stick) butter, softened
1/2	cup packed brown sugar
1	cup sifted all-purpose flour

1/4 cup quick-cooking oats
1/4 cup finely chopped walnuts
Assorted chopped or sliced fruits such as
strawberries, grapes, kiwifruit,
oranges, canned or fresh pineapple,
bananas, cantaloupe and/or
honeydew melon

Whisk the condensed milk, sour cream, lemon juice and vanilla in a bowl until blended. Chill, covered, in the refrigerator.

Beat the butter and brown sugar in a mixing bowl until light and fluffy. Add the flour, oats and walnuts and mix well. Press the oat mixture into a 12-inch round with a rim on a lightly oiled pizza pan. Bake at 375 degrees for 10 to 12 minutes or until golden brown. Cool on a wire rack. Spread the chilled condensed milk mixture over the crust and top with the desired fruit. Chill and cut into wedges.

SERVES 6

BANANA SPLIT CAKE

2 cups graham cracker crumbs
1/2 cup (1 stick) butter, melted
1 (1-pound) package 10x confectioners' sugar
1 cup (2 sticks) butter, softened
2 eggs

2 (15-ounce) cans crushed pineapple, drained
4 or 5 bananas, sliced
3 (16-ounce) packages frozen sliced strawberries, thawed and drained
1 cup heavy whipping cream, whipped
1/2 cup chopped pecans

Mix the graham cracker crumbs and 1/2 cup melted butter in a bowl. Press the crumb mixture over the bottom of a 9x13-inch dish. Beat the confectioners' sugar, 1 cup butter and the eggs in a mixing bowl for 12 minutes, scraping the bowl occasionally. Pour over the prepared layer and chill, covered, for 4 hours.

Layer the pineapple, bananas and strawberries over the prepared layers in the order listed. Spread with the whipped cream and sprinkle with the pecans. Chill, covered, in the refrigerator. Drizzle with hot fudge sauce or chocolate sauce if desired.

If you are concerned about using raw eggs, use eggs pasteurized in their shells, which are sold at some specialty food stores, or use an equivalent amount of pasteurized egg substitute.

SERVES 12

WORTH TASTING

CHOCOLATY CHOCOLATE CAKE

CAKE
1 cup skim milk

1 tablespoon lemon juice

1³/4 cups unbleached all-purpose flour

2 cups sugar

³/4 cup baking cocoa

2 teaspoons baking soda

1 teaspoon baking powder

1 teaspoon salt

1 cup strong black coffee, cooled

¹/2 cup vegetable oil

1 teaspoon vanilla extract

2 eggs

CHOCOLATE FROSTING
4 ounces unsweetened chocolate

¹/2 cup (1 stick) unsalted butter

1 (1-pound) package confectioners' sugar

¹/2 cup evaporated milk

1 teaspoon vanilla extract

¹/8 teaspoon salt

To prepare the cake, line two 9-inch cake pans with baking parchment and dust lightly with flour. Mix the skim milk and lemon juice in a bowl. Whisk the flour, sugar, baking cocoa, baking soda, baking powder and salt in a mixing bowl. Add the milk mixture, coffee, oil, vanilla and eggs and beat at low speed until combined. Increase the speed to medium and beat for 2 minutes longer; the batter will be thin. Pour the batter into the prepared cake pans and bake at 350 degrees for 35 to 40 minutes or until the layers test done. Cool in the pans for 10 minutes and remove to a wire rack to cool completely.

To prepare the frosting, combine the chocolate and butter in a microwave-safe dish. Microwave at 30-second intervals until blended, stirring after each interval. Mix the confectioners' sugar, evaporated milk, vanilla and salt in a bowl using a wooden spoon until combined. Add the chocolate mixture and beat by hand until stiff. The frosting may have to be chilled and brought back to room temperature to obtain a frosting consistency. Spread the frosting between the layers and over the top and side of the cake. Store, covered, at room temperature.

SERVES 8 TO 12

Cocoa butter is the vegetable fat content of the cocoa bean. The edible part of the bean is roasted, ground, and liquefied into a chocolate liquor. Following are the different types of chocolate. BITTER CHOCOLATE *or* UNSWEETENED CHOCOLATE *is 53 percent cocoa butter. It is used for baking and is also called baking chocolate.* BITTERSWEET *or* SEMISWEET CHOCOLATE *is slightly sweetened. It is also called dark chocolate.* SWEET CHOCOLATE *has more sugar than semisweet chocolate, and milk chocolate contains sugar and milk. Both are used in decorating and making candy.* WHITE CHOCOLATE *contains no cocoa powder and cannot legally be called chocolate in the United States. It is technically white confectionary coating.*

WORTH TASTING

LAYERED JAM CAKE

CAKE

1¹/2 cups all-purpose flour
2 teaspoons baking powder
¹/4 teaspoon salt
1 cup heavy whipping cream
1 cup sifted sugar
2 eggs
1 teaspoon vanilla extract

FUDGE FROSTING AND ASSEMBLY

¹/2 cup (1 stick) butter
2 ounces unsweetened chocolate,
     chopped
2¹/2 cups (or more) confectioners' sugar
¹/2 cup (or more) light cream
2 teaspoons vanilla extract
¹/2 cup all-fruit apricot jam
¹/2 cup all-fruit raspberry jam

To prepare the cake, coat a 9-inch springform pan with butter and sprinkle lightly with sugar. Sift the flour, baking powder and salt together. Beat the whipping cream in a mixing bowl until thick but not stiff. Fold the sugar into the whipped cream with a rubber spatula. Whisk the eggs and vanilla in a bowl until blended and fold into the whipped cream mixture. Fold in the dry ingredients. Spoon the batter into the prepared pan and bake at 350 degrees for 35 minutes or until the top springs back when lightly touched and the cake pulls from the side of the pan. Cool in the pan for 15 minutes. Remove the side of the pan and cool the cake on a wire rack until room temperature.

To prepare the frosting, melt the butter and chocolate in a saucepan over low heat, stirring occasionally. Let stand until room temperature. Beat the confectioners' sugar, cream and vanilla in a mixing bowl until smooth. Add the chocolate mixture gradually, beating constantly at high speed until of a spreading consistency. Add additional cream for a thinner consistency and additional confectioners' sugar for a thicker consistency.

To assemble, cut the cake into three equal layers. Arrange the bottom layer on a cake plate and spread with half the apricot jam. Top with the middle layer and spread with the raspberry jam. Top with the remaining layer and spread with the remaining apricot jam. Spread two-thirds of the frosting over the side of the cake. Pipe the remaining frosting around the edge of the cake. Chill, covered, until set.

SERVES 12

The Aztec Indians were the originators of CHOCOLATE *as it was they
who combined the fruit of the cacao seeds with chili peppers to make a drink called chocolatl.
The Aztecs believed that cacao seeds came from Paradise and that you gained
wisdom from eating its fruit. When Spain invaded Mexico, they took cacao beans back to
Spain and began to harvest them. They added sugar instead of chili peppers and
called the drink cocoa. It was a hit in Spain and all over Europe.*

WORTH TASTING

GUAVA CAKE

2	cups all-purpose flour		1	cup granulated sugar
1	tablespoon baking powder		2	eggs
1/4	teaspoon salt		1	pound guava paste, cut into 16 slices
1/2	cup (1 stick) butter			Confectioners' sugar
2	tablespoons vegetable lard			

Sift the flour, baking powder and salt together twice. Beat the butter, lard and granulated sugar in a mixing bowl until light and fluffy, scraping the bowl occasionally. Add the dry ingredients and mix well. Add the eggs one at a time, mixing well after each addition.

Spoon half the batter into a greased 8×8-inch glass baking dish or aluminum baking pan. Top with the guava paste slices and spread with the remaining batter. Bake at 350 degrees for 40 to 45 minutes or until the edges pull from the sides of the dish. Cool in the dish on a wire rack. Sprinkle with confectioner's sugar and cut into sixteen squares just before serving.

SERVES 8

GUAVAS are small tropical fruits, the flavor of which resembles strawberries.
They are great for making jams, jellies, and preserves. Guava paste can be
found in the ethnic section of your local grocery store, or at a Hispanic market.

HEATH BAR DREAM CAKE

1	(2-layer) package German chocolate cake mix		1	cup caramel sauce
1	cup (6 ounces) milk chocolate chips		12	ounces whipped topping
1	(14-ounce) can sweetened condensed milk		3	Heath bars, crushed

Prepare the cake using the package directions for a 9×11-inch cake pan. Bake for 10 minutes and sprinkle with the chocolate chips. Continue baking until the cake tests done. Remove from the oven and immediately pierce the top of the hot cake with the handle of a wooden spoon or spatula.

Pour the condensed milk over the top of the cake. Chill for 1 hour or until cool. Spread the caramel sauce and whipping topping over the prepared layers and sprinkle with the candy bars. Store, covered, in the refrigerator until serving time.

SERVES 12

WORTH TASTING

JACK'S FAVORITE CAKE

CAKE

2	cups all-purpose flour
1 1/2	cups sugar
1	teaspoon baking soda
1	teaspoon salt
1	teaspoon ground cinnamon
1	teaspoon ground nutmeg
1	cup vegetable oil
1/2	cup buttermilk
3	eggs
1	cup stewed pitted prunes, chopped
1	cup chopped pecans
1	teaspoon vanilla extract

BUTTERMILK SAUCE AND ASSEMBLY

1	cup sugar
1/2	cup (1 stick) butter
1/2	cup buttermilk
1	teaspoon baking soda

To prepare the cake, sift the flour, sugar, baking soda, salt, cinnamon and nutmeg into a bowl and mix well. Add the oil, buttermilk and eggs and mix well. Stir in the prunes, pecans and vanilla. Pour the batter into a greased and floured 9×13-inch cake pan and bake at 350 degrees for 30 to 40 minutes or until the edges pull from the sides of the pan.

To prepare the sauce, combine the sugar, butter, buttermilk and baking soda in a saucepan and bring to a boil, stirring constantly.

To assemble, pierce the top of the warm cake in several places with a fork. Pour the warm sauce over the cake. Cool in the pan on a wire rack and cut into eighteen 2×3-inch pieces. This rich moist cake is a special nineteenth-hole treat of golfer Jack Nicklaus.

SERVES 18

Barbara Nicklaus, who submitted this recipe, is a Junior League of the Palm Beaches sustainer and a recipe contributor to the League's three previous cookbooks, Palm Beach Entertains, Heart of the Palms, *and* Slice of Paradise.

WORTH TASTING

BROWN SUGAR POUND CAKE

CAKE

3	cups sifted all-purpose flour
1	teaspoon baking powder
1/2	teaspoon salt
1	cup (2 sticks) butter
1/2	cup vegetable oil
1	cup granulated sugar
1	(1-pound) package light brown sugar
5	eggs
1	cup milk
1	teaspoon vanilla extract
1	cup chopped nuts

BROWN SUGAR GLAZE

1/2	cup packed brown sugar
2	tablespoons vegetable oil
2	tablespoons butter
2	tablespoons milk
1/2	teaspoon salt
1	teaspoon vanilla extract
Chopped nuts to taste	

To prepare the cake, sift the flour, baking powder and salt together. Combine the butter and oil in a large mixing bowl. Gradually add the granulated sugar and brown sugar to the butter mixture gradually, beating constantly until light and fluffy. Add the eggs one at a time, beating well after each addition. Add the dry ingredients alternately with the milk, mixing well after each addition. Blend in the vanilla and stir in the nuts. Spoon the batter into a greased 10-inch tube pan and bake at 350 degrees for 1 1/4 hours. Cool in the pan for 10 minutes and remove to a heatproof platter.

To prepare the glaze, bring the brown sugar, oil, butter, milk and salt to a boil in a saucepan, stirring occasionally. Remove from the heat and stir in the vanilla and nuts. Pour the hot glaze over the warm cake and broil until bubbly and light brown. Let stand until cool.

SERVES 16

This tried-and-true favorite has appeared in Heart of the Palms *and* Slice of Paradise.

WORTH TASTING

RUM CAKE

CAKE

1	(2-layer) yellow cake mix with pudding
1/2	cup water
1/2	cup vegetable oil
1/2	cup light rum
4	eggs

RUM GLAZE AND ASSEMBLY

1	cup sugar
1/2	cup (1 stick) butter
1/2	cup light rum
1/2	cup water

To prepare the cake, combine the cake mix, water, oil, rum and eggs in a mixing bowl and beat until blended. Pour the batter into a greased and floured tube pan. Bake at 325 degrees for 50 to 60 minutes or until the cake tests done.

To prepare the glaze, bring the sugar, butter, rum and water to a boil in a saucepan. Boil for 2 to 5 minutes or to the desired consistency, stirring occasionally. Invert the cake onto a cake plate and pierce the top of the hot cake with a wooden pick. Pour the hot glaze over the cake and let stand until cool.

SERVES 12

WHISKEY CAKE

1	(2-layer) package yellow cake mix
1	(2-ounce) package butterscotch instant pudding mix
1/2	cup vegetable oil
1/2	cup water
1/2	cup whiskey
4	eggs
1	(2-ounce) package chocolate instant pudding mix

1	(2-layer) package chocolate cake mix
1/2	cup vegetable oil
1/2	cup water
1/2	cup whiskey
4	eggs
2	cups sugar
1	cup (2 sticks) butter
1/2	cup water
1	cup whiskey

Combine the yellow cake mix, butterscotch pudding mix, 1/2 cup oil, 1/2 cup water, 1/2 cup whiskey and 4 eggs in a mixing bowl and beat until blended. Pour equal amounts of the batter into two nonstick bundt pans. Beat the chocolate pudding mix, chocolate cake mix, 1/2 cup oil, 1/2 cup water, 1/2 cup whiskey and 4 eggs in a mixing bowl until blended. Pour equal amounts of the batter over the prepared layers. Bake at 350 degrees for 45 minutes or until the cakes test done.

Combine the sugar, butter and 1/2 cup water in a saucepan and bring to a boil, stirring occasionally. Stir in 1 cup whiskey. Pour the hot whiskey mixture over the hot cakes and let stand until cool.

MAKES 2 CAKES

WORTH TASTING

PUMPKIN ROLL

CAKE
1 cup sugar

3/4 cup all-purpose flour

1 teaspoon baking soda

1/2 teaspoon ground cinnamon

2/3 cup pumpkin purée

3 eggs, lightly beaten

CREAM CHEESE FILLING
AND ASSEMBLY
8 ounces cream cheese, softened

1 cup confectioners' sugar

2 tablespoons butter

3/4 teaspoon vanilla extract

To prepare the cake, combine the sugar, flour, baking soda and cinnamon in a bowl and mix well. Add the pumpkin and eggs and mix until blended. Spread the batter on a jelly roll pan lined with waxed paper. Bake at 350 degrees for 15 minutes.

Moisten a clean kitchen towel and squeeze out the excess water until just slightly damp. Lay the damp towel over the jelly roll pan and invert the cake onto the towel. Peel off the waxed paper. Roll the warm cake in the towel as for a jelly roll. Cool on a wire rack for 1 hour.

To prepare the filling, beat the cream cheese, confectioners' sugar, butter and vanilla in a mixing bowl until of a spreading consistency, scraping the bowl occasionally.

To assemble, unroll the cake carefully and remove the towel. Spread the filling to within 1 inch of the edge and reroll. Chill, covered, until serving time.

SERVES 10

GRAHAM CRACKER MAGIC BARS

1 cup graham cracker crumbs

1/2 cup (1 stick) butter, melted

1 cup chopped walnuts

1 cup (6 ounces) chocolate chips

1 cup shredded coconut

1 (14-ounce) can sweetened
condensed milk

Toss the graham cracker crumbs and butter in a bowl. Pat the crumb mixture over the bottom of a 9×13-inch baking pan. Layer the walnuts, chocolate chips and coconut over the prepared layer. Pour the condensed milk evenly over the top.

Bake at 350 degrees for 30 minutes or until golden brown. Let stand until cool and cut into 2-inch bars. Pour additional condensed milk over the top for a chewier texture.

MAKES 2 DOZEN BARS

TURTLE BROWNIE BARS

1	(2-layer) package German chocolate cake mix	1/3	cup sweetened condensed milk
2/3	cup sweetened condensed milk	1	cup chopped pecans
3/4	cup (1 1/2 sticks) butter, melted	1	cup (6 ounces) semisweet chocolate chips
1	(12-ounce) package caramels		

Combine the cake mix, 2/3 cup condensed milk and the butter in a bowl and mix well. Spread half the cake mix mixture over the bottom of an 11×15-inch baking pan. Bake at 350 degrees for 15 minutes. Maintain the oven temperature.

Heat the caramels in a saucepan over low heat until melted, stirring occasionally. Add 1/3 cup condensed milk and stir until blended. Pour the caramel mixture over the baked layer and sprinkle with the pecans and chocolate chips. Spread the remaining cake mix mixture as evenly as possible over the prepared layers and bake for 20 minutes. Let stand until cool and then cut into bars.

MAKES 3 TO 4 DOZEN BARS

RASPBERRY-FILLED WHITE CHOCOLATE BARS

1	cup (2 sticks) butter	1	teaspoon salt
2	cups (12 ounces) white chocolate chips	1	teaspoon almond extract
4	eggs	2	cups (12 ounces) white chocolate chips
1	cup sugar	1	cup seedless raspberry preserves
2	cups all-purpose flour	1/2	cup sliced almonds

Melt the butter in a saucepan over low heat and add 2 cups white chocolate chips; do not stir. Beat the eggs in a mixing bowl until foamy. Add the sugar gradually to the eggs, beating constantly at high speed until pale yellow in color. Stir in the white chocolate chip mixture. Add the flour, salt and flavoring and beat at low speed just until combined. Spread half the batter in a greased and floured 9×13-inch baking pan. Bake at 325 degrees for 10 to 15 minutes or until golden brown. Maintain the oven temperature.

Stir 2 cups white chocolate chips into the remaining batter. Spoon the preserves into a microwave-safe dish and microwave until melted. Spread the preserves over the baked layer and gently spoon the remaining batter over the preserves. Sprinkle with the almonds and bake for 30 minutes longer. Cool in the pan on a wire rack and then cut into bars. To make removal easier, line the baking pan with baking parchment.

MAKES 2 DOZEN BARS

SEVEN LAYERS OF SIN BARS

^{1}/2 cup (1 stick) butter, melted
1^1/2 cups graham cracker crumbs
1 cup (6 ounces) chocolate chips
1 cup (6 ounces) butterscotch chips
1 cup chopped pecans
1 cup flaked coconut
1 (14-ounce) can sweetened
    condensed milk

Pour the butter into a 9×13-inch baking pan, tilting the pan to ensure even coverage. Sprinkle the graham cracker crumbs over the butter. Layer with the chocolate chips, butterscotch chips, pecans and coconut in the order listed. Pour the condensed milk over the top and bake at 350 degrees for 25 minutes. Let stand until cool and then cut into bars.

MAKES 2 TO 3 DOZEN BARS

CHOCOLATE CHIPS *were invented by Mrs. Ruth Wakefield in 1937*
when she ran out of baking chocolate and substituted broken pieces of semisweet
chocolate in her cookie dough. She owned the Toll House Inn in Massachusetts,
hence the name Toll House Cookies for chocolate chips cookies.

DOUBLE-CHOCOLATE BROWNIES

1 (21-ounce) package fudge
    brownie mix
^{3}/4 cup milk
^{1}/4 cup vegetable oil
1 egg, beaten
^{1}/4 cup prepared instant hot chocolate
^{3}/4 cup milk chocolate baking pieces
^{3}/4 cup white chocolate baking pieces
^{1}/2 cup semisweet chocolate
    baking pieces
^{1}/2 cup chopped walnuts or pecans
    (optional)

Combine the brownie mix, milk, oil, egg and hot chocolate in a bowl and stir with a wooden spoon until blended. Add the milk chocolate pieces, white chocolate pieces, semisweet chocolate pieces and walnuts and stir just until combined.

Spread the batter in a greased 9×13-inch baking pan and bake at 350 degrees for 30 minutes. Cool in the pan on a wire rack and then cut into bars.

MAKES 2 DOZEN BROWNIES

WORTH TASTING

CHOCOLATE CARAMEL BROWNIES

1	cup all-purpose flour	1	teaspoon vanilla extract
2/3	cup baking cocoa	1	(14-ounce) package caramels
2	cups (4 sticks) margarine, softened	1/2	cup evaporated milk
2	cups sugar	1	cup (6 ounces) semisweet
4	eggs		chocolate pieces

Mix the flour and baking cocoa in a bowl. Beat the margarine and sugar in a mixing bowl until creamy, scraping the bowl occasionally. Add the eggs one at a time, beating well after each addition. Mix in the flour mixture until blended. Add the vanilla and beat until smooth. Spread half the batter in a greased 9×13-inch baking pan and bake at 350 degrees for 5 minutes. Maintain the oven temperature.

Combine the caramels and evaporated milk in a double boiler and heat over low heat until blended, stirring occasionally. Remove from the heat. Sprinkle the chocolate pieces over the baked layer and drizzle with the caramel mixture. Drop the remaining batter by small spoonfuls over the prepared layers and spread evenly using the back of a spoon. Bake for 25 to 35 minutes or until the edges pull from the sides of the pan. Cool in the pan on a wire rack. Chill for 30 minutes and then cut into bars.

MAKES 2 TO 3 DOZEN BROWNIES

STRAWBERRY MUD

1	(21-ounce) package brownie mix	1/2	teaspoon strawberry extract
1	cup sifted confectioners' sugar	3	or 4 drops of red food coloring
2	tablespoons butter, softened	2	ounces semisweet chocolate
1	tablespoon milk	2	tablespoons butter

Prepare the brownies using the package directions for a 9×13-inch baking pan. Cool in the pan on a wire rack. Combine the confectioners' sugar, 2 tablespoons butter, the milk, flavoring and food coloring in a mixing bowl and beat until smooth. Spread over the top of the cooled baked layer. Chill in the refrigerator until firm.

Melt the chocolate and 2 tablespoons butter in a saucepan over low heat, stirring occasionally. Spread the chocolate mixture over the cooled layers. Let stand until set and then cut into bars.

MAKES 2 TO 3 DOZEN BARS

WORTH TASTING

GINGER COOKIES

2	cups all-purpose flour	1	cup sugar
2	teaspoons baking soda	3/4	cup shortening
1	teaspoon each ground cinnamon,	1/4	cup molasses
	cloves and ginger	1	egg
1/16	teaspoon salt		Sugar for coating

Mix the flour, baking soda, cinnamon, cloves, ginger and salt in a bowl. Beat 1 cup sugar and the shortening in a mixing bowl until creamy. Add the molasses and egg to the creamed mixture and beat until blended. Add the flour mixture gradually, beating constantly until smooth. Chill, covered, for 2 hours.

Shape the dough into small balls and coat with sugar. Arrange the balls on a cookie sheet and bake at 375 degrees for 10 minutes. Cool on the cookie sheet for 2 minutes and remove to a wire rack to cool completely. Store in an airtight container.

MAKES 2 DOZEN COOKIES

In the United Kingdom, a COOKIE *is referred to as a biscuit. In the United States, cookies are found in many shapes:* BAR COOKIES *are soft and cake-like, like a brownie.* MOLDED COOKIES *have a shape.* ROLLED COOKIES *are thin and crisp.* BALLED COOKIES *are rolled into balls and usually coated with sugar and/or nuts.*

WALNUT CINNAMON BALLS

1 1/2	cups all-purpose flour	1/2	cup (1 stick) butter, softened
1/2	teaspoon baking powder	2	eggs, or 4 egg yolks
1/4	teaspoon salt		Ground walnuts to taste
1	cup sugar		Ground cinnamon to taste

Sift the flour, baking powder and salt together. Beat the sugar and butter in a mixing bowl until creamy. Add the eggs to the creamed mixture and beat until blended. Add the flour mixture and beat until smooth. Chill, covered, for 1 hour. Shape the dough into 1-inch balls and coat with a mixture of ground walnuts and cinnamon. Arrange the coated balls 1-inch apart on a cookie sheet sprayed with nonstick cooking spray. Bake at 375 degrees for 12 minutes. Cool on the cookie sheet for 2 minutes. Remove to a wire rack to cool completely. Store in an airtight container.

MAKES 3 DOZEN COOKIES

WORTH TASTING

KEY LIME PIE

1 package graham cracker crust mix	Grated zest of 1 Key lime
8 ounces cream cheese, softened	1/2 cup heavy whipping cream
1 (14-ounce) can sweetened	2 teaspoons confectioners' sugar
condensed milk	1 teaspoon vanilla extract
1/2 cup Key lime juice	Toasted coconut (optional)
1 teaspoon vanilla extract	

Prepare the graham cracker crust using the package directions, baking for 8 minutes. Let stand until cool and then chill for 1 hour.

Beat the cream cheese and condensed milk in a mixing bowl until smooth. Add the lime juice, 1 teaspoon vanilla and the lime zest and beat until combined. Spoon the cream cheese mixture over the baked layer. Beat the whipping cream in a mixing bowl until soft peaks form. Add the confectioners' sugar and 1 teaspoon vanilla and beat until combined. Spread the whipped cream over the top of the pie, sealing to the edge. Sprinkle with coconut. Chill, covered, until serving time.

SERVES 6 TO 8

In 2006 the Florida legislature declared Key Lime Pie the official Florida state pie.

MILLION DOLLAR PIE

GRAHAM CRACKER CRUST

1 1/4 cups graham cracker crumbs
5 tablespoons sugar
1/2 cup (1 stick) margarine, melted

PIE

1 (20-ounce) can crushed
   pineapple, drained
1 (14-ounce) can sweetened
   condensed milk
10 ounces extra creamy whipped topping
5 tablespoons lemon juice

To prepare the crust, mix the graham cracker crumbs and sugar in a bowl. Add the margarine and stir until coated. Press the crumb mixture over the bottom and up the side of a 9-inch pie plate.

To prepare the pie, combine the pineapple, condensed milk, whipped topping and lemon juice in a bowl and mix well. Spoon the pineapple mixture into the prepared pie plate and chill, covered, for 4 hours or longer.

SERVES 8

WORTH TASTING

PEANUT BUTTER PIE

4	ounces cream cheese, softened	1/3	cup peanut butter
1	cup confectioners' sugar	8	ounces whipped topping
1/2	cup milk	1	(9-inch) graham cracker pie shell

Beat the cream cheese and confectioners' sugar in a mixing bowl until smooth. Beat the milk and peanut butter in a mixing bowl until blended. Add the peanut butter mixture to the cream cheese mixture and mix well. Fold in the whipped topping.

Spoon the peanut butter mixture into the pie shell and freeze, covered, until firm. A delicious addition to Thanksgiving dinner, or a great substitution for the usual birthday cake.

SERVES 8 TO 10

PEACHES AND CREAM CHEESE PIE

1	(20-ounce) can sliced peaches	1	teaspoon baking powder
3/4	cup all-purpose flour	1/2	teaspoon salt
1/2	cup milk	8	ounces cream cheese, softened
1	(3-ounce) package vanilla instant pudding mix	1/2	cup sugar
3	tablespoons margarine, softened	1/2	teaspoon ground cinnamon
1	egg	1	tablespoon sugar

Drain the peaches, reserving 3 tablespoons of the juice. Combine the flour, milk, pudding mix, margarine, egg, baking powder and salt in a mixing bowl. Beat at medium speed for 2 minutes, scraping the bowl occasionally. Pour into a greased pie plate and arrange the peaches over the top.

Combine the cream cheese, 1/2 cup sugar and the reserved peach juice in a mixing bowl. Beat at medium speed until creamy. Spoon the cream cheese mixture over the prepared layers. Mix the cinnamon and 1 tablespoon sugar in a small bowl and sprinkle over the top. Bake at 350 degrees for 30 to 35 minutes.

SERVES 8

OUTDOOR LIVING *and* DINING, *a staple of life in Palm Beach to this day, was expressed in the design of many Mediterranean Revival estate homes in Palm Beach. In luxurious taste, several of these homes boast not one, but two outdoor dining loggias, or colonnades. These shaded spaces not only helped to cool the pre-air-conditioned homes of the Palm Beach elite, but they also maximized outdoor dining options; one loggia was enjoyed for breakfast, and the other for lunch.*

WORTH TASTING

Acknowledgments

The Junior League of the Palm Beaches expresses grateful appreciation to the following businesses and members who through their generous donations made *Worth Tasting* possible.

We Thank Our **Benefactor**:
LaBovick, LaBovick, & Wald, P.A.

We Thank Our **Sponsors**:
The Breakers Hotel
Northern Trust Bank

We Thank Our **Contributors**:
Dawn Burkhead
Mary Hulitar
Kelly Layman
Patricia McConnell
Kathryn Vecellio
Barbara Williamson

The Junior League of the Palm beaches thanks the following members, friends, and businesses who contributed the time, energy, creativity and guidance that helped to make *Worth Tasting* a beautiful cookbook.

Gregory Ross, Ross Studios
FRP and its wonderful editors and mentors
Kelly Tracht for her beautiful cover
Brenda Lusher, owner, founder, and designer of Mizner Industries for the use of her tiles
Barbara Nicklaus for her wonderful introduction
The National Croquet Center for its continued support of The Junior League of the Palm Beaches
Virginia Philip, Master Sommelier, The Breakers Hotel, for her wine pairings
Amy Pagan for getting us started
Ann Gagliardi for all her hard work during the transition phase

The Junior League of the Palm Beaches thanks the following sites for allowing us on their respective premises for photography purposes.

Ann Norton House and Sculpture Garden
The Breakers Hotel
The Harriet Himmel Theater
Mar-a-Lago

Seagull Cottage
The Society of the Four Arts
Via Mizner Industries
Worth Avenue

KELLY TRACHT

Kelly Tracht's love for all things tropical began in her childhood growing up in the charming Gulf coast beach town of Clearwater, Florida. She pursued her undergraduate studies in architecture at the University of Florida, where she had the opportunity to live and study abroad in Vicenza, Italy. Sketching from the great Renaissance masters such as Michelangelo and Raphael fueled her love of art, and after graduation Kelly went on to pursue art professionally, living and working on the Caribbean island of Grenada. It was there that she was able to sell her first landscape painting.

Upon her return to the United States, Kelly worked in various architectural firms and continued to pursue art. She studied with well-known classical painters, which led to several professional portrait commissions. In 2001, she was awarded a scholarship to continue her architectural studies and went on to earn her Masters of Architecture degree from Miami University of Ohio, where she met her husband, Rich. They now live and work in Tequesta, Florida, and collaborate on Conch- and Mediterranean-style custom residences for various clients throughout the state of Florida. Kelly is also continuing to pursue painting in the form of illustration, murals, and classical portraiture. She has been a member of The Junior League of the Palm Beaches since 2005.

Recipe Contributors

Worth Tasting would not have been possible without the wonderful input of
its members, friends, and families by testing hundreds of recipes and sharing fabulous recipes.
We thank the following recipe contributors and recipe testers.

Lynn Abney
Heather Andrews
Tami Augen
Julie Marie Augustyn
Stephanie Barimo
Denise A. Bas
Beth Beattie
Jenifer Blanks
Elizabeth Bockmeyer
Diane Bojovic
Shannon Brewer
Amy Royster Bridger
Carolyn Broadhead
Samantha Catanese
Carol Cestero
Shani Core
E.J. Crittenden
Blythe Crosby
Jane Dahlmeier
Kim Dahlmeier
Liza Debartolo
Morgan DeFranco
Carin Douglas
Janine Dubauskas
Marcy Duckworth
Michelle Faivre
Terri Fekete
Meaghan Flenner

Christine Frankhouser
Melissa Fritsch
Lisa Gallagher
Melissa Giardina
Lizet Guildford
Catherine Hennessey
Deanna Herbst
Lisa Huertas
Sabra Ingeman
Lisa Jaloski
Lori Johnson
Jennifer Jones
Krissy Kairalla
Maureen Kane
Allison Kapner
Pam Karagoz
Kecia Keller
Katy Kern
Anne Kirchhoff
Betty Ann Korst
Barda Kosovrasti
Esther Uria LaBovick
Jennifer Leo
Lisa Lettenmaier
Sharon Lewis
Carol Lucey
Katy Lynch
Kimberly Lyon

Janice Marshall
Cheryl Martell
Disa Mason
Patricia Evans McConnell
Lisa Mercado
Jackie Mercer
Kate Merrell
Gail Mills
Jennifer Morrison
Heather Neville
Barbara Nicklaus
Tina O'Brien
Amy Oliver
Jeannine Osborne
Amy Pagan
Yvonne Patterson
Julia Pichette
Jaimee S. Pierce
Melissa Pollock
Crissy Poorman
Jill Pritch
Amy Quattlebaum
Alice Randolph
Kristen Ray
Mary Reynolds
Kelly Ring
Jill Rose
Glory Ross

Lisa Russo
Anne Rutter
Jessica Savidge
Anita Schrubb
Alohalani Scott
Micah Scribner-Ford
Kristy Seibert
Tania Sigman
Laura Smeenge
Florence Stevens
Carolyn Stone
Deborah Sutera
Susan Teaford
Rena Toppe
Kelly Tracht
Amy Triggs
Leah G. Vincent
Snooky Vivien
Kelly Wandoff
Wilton White
Mari Whittlesey
Ione Wiren
Wendy Wells
Beverly Wingert
Kristen Wunder

Recipe Testers

Shelly Albright
Allyson Andres
Tami Augen
Denise A. Bas
Laura Burke
Shani Core
Dianna Craven
Blythe Crosby
Kim Dahlmeier
Tasha Dickinson
Holly Donaldson
Aime Dunstan
Terri Fekete
Samantha Feuer
Meaghan Flenner
Christine Frankhouser

Ann Gagliardi
Ashley Goins
Deanna Herbst
Lisa Huertas
Sabra Ingeman
Christine Jerabek
Christina Jordan
Allison Kapner
Mary Kilian
Jennifer Kypreos
Esther Uria LaBovick
Megan Laraway
Jennifer Leo
Sharon Lewis
Denise Long
Kimberly Lyon

Jill MacPherson
Susan Mayes
Amy McGill
Monica Merchant
Kate Merrell
Jennifer Morrison
Janet Murphy
Tina O'Brien
Robyn O'Reilly
Susan Oyer
Amy Pagan
Rebecca Patterson
Yvonne Patterson
Lynda Pepper
Emily Perrotto
Cami Preti

Jill Pritch
Alice Randolph
Kim Reed
Mary Reynolds
Jill Rose
Anne Rundels
Anne Rutter
Jessica Savidge
Alohalani Scott
Nicole Stevens
Deborah Sutera
Susan Teaford
Amy Triggs
Christine Walter
Sarah White
Mari Whittelsey

Bibliography

Ash, Jennifer. *Private Palm Beach: Tropical Style*. Abbeville Press, New York, 1992.

The Breakers Hotel. June 15, 2006, http://www.thebreakers.com.

Chalmers, Irena. *The Great Food Almanac*. Collins Publishers San Francisco. San Francisco, California, 1994.

City Place. June 15, 2006, http://www.cityplace.com/.

Curl, Donald. *Mizner's Florida: American Resort Architecture*. The Architectural History Foundation, New York. The MIT Press, Cambridge, Massachusetts, and London, 1984.

Curl, Donald W., Editor. *Palm Beach County: In a Class by Itself*. Copperfield Publications, Ft. Lauderdale, 1998.

Earl, Polly Ann. *Palm Beach: An Architectural Legacy*. Rizzoli, New York, 2002, 2003.

Flagler Museum. April 17, 2006. http://www.flagler.org/.

The Food Timeline: History Notes-Bread. http://www.foodtimeline.org/foodbreads.html.

Harmon, John E. *Atlas of Popular Culture in the Northeastern U.S.* http://www.geography.ccsu_edu/harmonj/atlas/buffwing.

Japanese Garden Research Network, Inc. (2006). Society of the Four Arts. Retrieved April 20, 2006, from www.jgarden.org.

Johnston, Shirley. *Palm Beach Houses*. Rizzoli, New York, 1991.

Mellgren, James. *All Cheese Considered: Blue Cheeses*, http://www.gourmetretailer.com/gourmetretailer/search/article_display.jsp?vnu_content_id=1001000574, VNU eMedia Inc., 2005.

Norris, Jan. *The Official Florida Dessert? Keylime Pie*. The Palm Beach Post. West Palm Beach, Florida, May 18, 2006.

O'Sullivan, Maureen. *Palm Beach: Then and Now*. Lickle Publishing Inc., West Palm Beach, 2004.

Seebohm, Caroline. *Boca Rococo: How Addison Mizner Invented Florida's Gold Coast*. Clarkson Potter Publishers, New York, 2001.

Shpritz, Dianna and O'Sullivan, Maureen. *Palm Beach: Then and Now*. Historical Society of Palm Beach and Lickle Publishing Inc., West Palm Beach, 2004.

Society of Four Arts. (2004). *Welcome to the Society of Four Arts*. Retrieved April 20, 2006, from www.fourarts.org.

Stradley, Linda. *What's Cooking America*. http://whatscookingamerica.net/glossary. 2006.

Waitrose Glossary, http://www.waitrose.com/.

Wikipedia. *The Free Encyclopedia*. http://en.wikipedia.org/w/index.php?title, and http://en.wikipedia.org/wiki/.

Worth Avenue. April 17, 2006. http://www.worth-avenue.com/.

http://plantanswers.tamu.edu/vegetables/leek.html.

WORTH TASTING

Menu Wines

Cocktail Party

PINOT NOIR, CALIFORNIA OR OREGON

Pinot Noir rarely disappoints, but use a bit of caution when choosing a Pinot Noir from California or Oregon versus Burgundy. The fruit and oak profiles are typically much different, and the Burgundies usually have more earth and mineral in them. Pinot Noir is made from a thin-skin grape and is known for its red fruit forwardness and racy acidity. For dishes with a bit more sweetness, such as the Crab Claws Coconut, the ripe fruit in this Pinot works great. The weight of the wine has just enough longevity to stand up to the Kalamata Olive Tapenade, yet will not overpower the rest of the menu.

Sunday Brunch

NONVINTAGE CHAMPAGNE

Why wait for a special day to drink bubbly? Everyday is special, and no other wine puts a smile on a face the way a great glass of Champagne can…Eighty-five percent of all Champagne made is nonvintage, or does not come from any particular year. The wines, by law, must be aged for a minimum of fifteen months. It requires a very skilled winemaker to make the blend (assemblage) taste the same each year as he/she may have as many as seventy base wines to blend from. Champagne's racy acidity and brioche notes allow it to pair with a variety of dishes and work very well with food served at brunch.

Ladies That Lunch

RIESLING, MOSEL-SAAR-RUWER, GERMANY

Riesling is on a swift comeback. Wines made from Riesling can age for decades, and no other country produces Rieslings of such elegance and finesse as Germany. The Mosel-Saar-Ruwer is known for its dramatic, slate slopes leading down to the Saar, Mosel, and Ruwer rivers. The sun reflects off the water each day and onto the slate soil, retaining heat. During the evening, when the nights become cool, the heat generated from the sun during the day radiates off the slate, moderating the temperature of the vines and allowing for even ripening of the grapes. Riesling has the ability to pair with a variety of dishes, including those with an Asian or Indian flair.

Bal Poudré Formal Supper

MEURSAULT, BURGUNDY, FRANCE

Made from the Chardonnay grape, this wine is the quintessential expression of fine Chardonnay. Butter, mineral, and hazelnuts marry together with an elegance and finesse that allows this wine to pair well with tricky dishes such as Sautéed Brussels Sprouts and Pesto Goat Cheese Dip.

CABERNET SAUVIGNON, NAPA, CALIFORNIA

Napa Valley Cabernet Sauvignon ranks among the best in the world. Full-bodied with ripe fruit flavors of blackberry, blueberry, and cassis, the fruit forwardness of this wine pairs well with beef, lamb, and game. Usually approachable at a younger age than its Bordeaux counterparts, even George Washington would be proud at this American icon of a wine.

Alfresco Grill-Out

FIANO DI AVELLINO, CAMPANIA, ITALY

Campania has a unique *terroir* and is known for using ancient grape varietals in their wines. The indigenous grapes Fiano di Avellino are sourced from the finest vineyards set in the rolling hills of the Irpinia region, located in close proximity to Mount Vesuvius. Medium-bodied with notes of apricot, lemon, and Granny Smith apple, this wine is bone-dry.

Island Party

ALBARIÑO, RIAS BAIXAS, SPAIN

The Albariño grape is often thought to be a distant relative to the Riesling grape. Due to its high quality and extreme scarcity, as well as being one of Spain's most expensive grapes, Albariño remained virtually unknown until the 1980s. A medium-bodied wine with peach, pear, and citrus notes, enhanced by the white floral nose and palate.

Gallery Night A Palette of Taste

CHIANTI, CLASSICO, TUSCANY

Chianti is divided into eight sub-districts. The Classico area of Chianti is considered to be the heart of the Chianti district. The wine is made predominately from Sangiovese, but can have the addition of white grapes such as Canaiolo, Trebbiano, and Malvasia. Up to 20 percent international grapes, such as Cabernet Sauvignon, are allowed as well. "Riserva" on a label indicates an additional aging of two years and three months. Medium-bodied with notes of cranberry, red cherry, and plum, the tannin and structure in this wine is just right for the Prime Rib, Spring Risotto, and Pesto Sauce.

Garden Tea Party

PINOT GRIS, ALSACE, FRANCE

Alsace is the only A.O.C. wine region in France that allows the grape varietal to be placed on the label. Pinot Gris is the same grape varietal as Pinot Grigio, but in Alsace, the continental climate and hilly terrain allows for a rounder and more lush style. No other country can replicate Alsace's unique style of Pinot Gris, or Riesling for that matter. Lush golden Delicious apple, lemon, and melon notes allow this wine to complement each of the dishes in its own unique way.

WORTH TASTING

Index

WORTH TASTING

WORTH TASTING

For additional copies of

Worth Tasting

Please contact:
The Junior League of the Palm Beaches
470 Columbia Drive, Building F
West Palm Beach, Florida 33409
561.689.7590

$29.95 plus $5.00 postage and handling per book.
Florida residents add 6.5% tax,
other states add current respective state tax.

The Junior League of the Palm Beaches accepts Visa and MasterCard.
Make personal checks payable to The Junior League of the Palm Beaches.